Developing Mathematical Ideas

Number and Operations, Part 3

Reasoning Algebraically About Operations

Casebook

A collaborative project by the staff and
participants of Teaching to the Big Ideas

Principal Investigators
Deborah Schifter
Virginia Bastable
Susan Jo Russell

With
Stephen Monk

And teacher collaborators

A new version of Reasoning Algebraically About Operations, *which highlights the* Common Core *content and mathematical practice standards, will be published by the National Council of Teachers of Mathematics.*

Go to <u>*http://mathleadership.org*</u> *to find out about DMI facilitation institutes and online DMI seminars offered by Mathematic Leadership programs at Mount Holyoke College.*

This work was supported by the National Science Foundation under Grant Nos. ESI-9254393 (awarded to EDC), ESI-9731064 (awarded to EDC), ESI-0095450 (awarded to TERC), and ESI-0242609 (awarded to EDC). Any opinions, findings, conclusions, or recommendations expressed here are those of the authors and do not necessarily reflect the views of the National Science Foundation.

Additional support was provided by a grant from the ExxonMobil Foundation.

"Number Line Capture" was developed by Susan Jo Russell, Deborah Schifter, and Virginia Bastable.

This book was previously published by: Pearson Education, Inc.

Cover photo credit: Mike Flynn

Teaching to the Big Ideas

Developing Mathematical Ideas (DMI) was developed as a collaborative project by the staff and participants of Teaching to the Big Ideas, an NSF Teacher Enhancement Project, and Investigations Revisions.

PROJECT DIRECTORS Deborah Schifter (Education Development Center), Virginia Bastable (SummerMath for Teachers at Mount Holyoke College), and Susan Jo Russell (TERC).

CONSULTANTS Elham Kazemi, Stephen Monk, Virginia Stimpson (University of Washington), Thomas Carpenter (University of Wisconsin at Madison), Herbert Clemens (Ohio State University), Mark Driscoll (Education Development Center), Benjamin Ford (Sonoma State University), Christopher Fraley (Lake Washington Public Schools), Megan Franke (University of California at Los Angeles), James Kaput (University of Massachusetts at Dartmouth), Jill Lester (Mount Holyoke College), James Lewis (University of Nebraska), Jean Moon (National Academy of Sciences), Loren Pitt (University of Virginia), Polly Wagner (Boston Public Schools), Erna Yackel (Purdue University at Calumet).

TEACHER COLLABORATORS Beth Alchek, Kim Beauregard, Barbara Bernard, Janelle Bradshaw, Nancy Buell, Mary Beth Cahill O'Connor, Rose Christiansen, Lisette Colon, Kim Cook, Fran Cooper, Maria D'Itria, Pat Erikson, Richard Feigenberg, Tom Fisher, Mike Flynn, Elaine Herzog, Kirsten Lee Howard, Liliana Klass, Melissa Lee, Jennifer Levitan, Solange Marsan, Kathe Millett, Florence Molyneaux, Elizabeth Monopoli, Robin Musser, Christine Norrman, Deborah Carey O'Brien, Anne Marie O'Reilly, Mark Paige, Crissy Pruitt, Margaret Riddle, Rebeka Eston Salemi, Karen Schweitzer, Lisa Seyferth, Geri Smith, Susan Bush Smith, Shoshy Starr, Elizabeth Sweeney, Janice Szymaszek, Danielle Thorne, Karen Tobin, JoAnn Traushke, Ana Vaisenstein, Carol Walker, Yvonne Watson-Murrell, Michelle Woods, and Mary Wright, representing the public schools of Amherst, Boston, Brookline, Cambridge, Greenfield, Holyoke, Lincoln, Natick, Newton, Northampton, South Hadley, Southampton, Springfield, Sudbury, Westwood, and Williamsburg, MA, and the Smith College Campus School in Northampton, MA.

VIDEO DEVELOPMENT David Smith (David Smith Productions)

FIELD TEST SITES Albuquerque Public Schools (New Mexico), Bedford County Public Schools (Virginia), Bismarck Public Schools (North Dakota), Boston Public Schools (Massachusetts), Buncombe County Public Schools (North Carolina), Durham Public Schools (North Carolina), Fayetteville Public Schools (Arkansas), Houston Independent School District (Texas), Lake Washington School District (Washington), Northampton Public Schools (Massachusetts), Seattle Public Schools (Washington), Stafford County Schools (Virginia), and Ventura Unified School District (California).

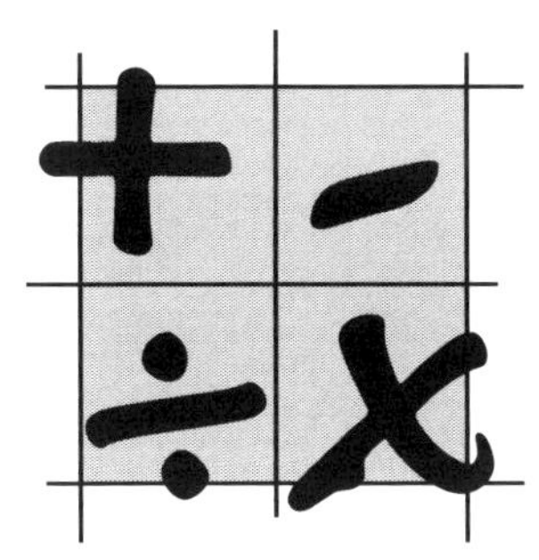

CONTENTS

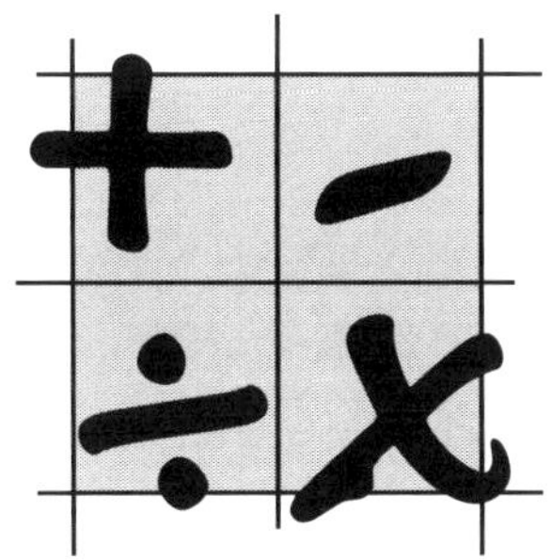

Introduction

For most adults, the use of letters to represent numbers—x's and y's—is the chief identifying feature of algebra. However, this notation in and of itself is only one aspect of algebraic thinking. The underlying reasoning about how operations work is what is critical to the understanding of algebra. This reasoning about operations is the aspect of algebra that is important work for elementary and middle-school students.

In *Number and Operations*, Part 1, *Building a System of Tens*, participants recognize how young students devise computational strategies for whole numbers and decimals. In *Number and Operations*, Part 2, *Making Meaning for Operations*, actions and situations modeled by the four basic operations are examined. *Number and Operations*, Part 3, *Reasoning Algebraically About Operations*, extends the work of the earlier modules to examine the generalizations students make about the operations and the reasoning entailed in addressing the question, "Does this always work?"[1]

For example, consider the following vignette:

> An elementary-grade class was exploring odd and even numbers. Several children noticed that whenever they added two even numbers, the result

[1] *Reasoning Algebraically About Operations* was written under the assumption that seminar participants will have already worked through the ideas of *Making Meaning for Operations.*

was an even number. Based on this evidence, several of the children were ready to declare that whenever you add any two even numbers, the sum is an even number. Others acknowledged that each time they tested it, it came out that way, but you cannot tell if it will always happen because "numbers go on forever."

Myra said she knows it will happen for all even numbers. Because, she said, if you take two even numbers, you can make them into pairs with none left over. Then, when you put the numbers together, you combine the parts so that your new number has pairs with none left over.

Myra illustrated what she meant with cubes and disks:

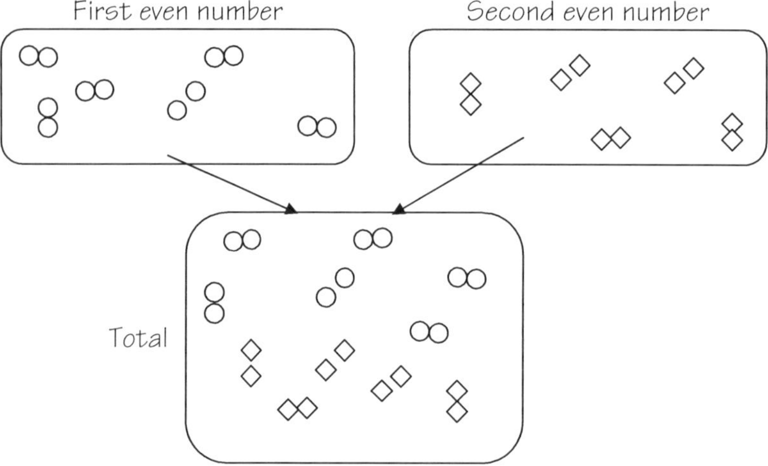

Felicity worked hard to understand what Myra had said. However, as she began to reiterate it, she went back to the idea that you can't know for all numbers. "There might be two even numbers somewhere that, when you add them together, make an odd. You just don't know."

Myra insisted she did know for all even numbers.

As students move from particular numbers and actions to *patterns of results*, they begin to make generalizations. That is, they begin to view numbers and operations as a system. This vignette illustrates a context in which students begin to notice generalizations and articulate what they see.

The vignette also raises several questions that will be explored in this module. What does it mean to make a generalization—a claim that something is *always* true? What does it mean to prove a generalization when making a claim about an infinite class of numbers and one cannot check every case? How do students engage with these questions and what constitutes "proof" at this level?

In this module, we will explore some of the generalizations that are central to our number system, generalizations that students can begin to explore in the context of their learning about numbers and computation. This module will cover three types of generalizations:

- Properties of operations: We take for granted that when two numbers are multiplied, the answer is the same no matter how we order the factors: $4 \times 6 = 6 \times 4$. To add 12 to any number, say 49, we automatically assume that the 12 can be broken into 10 and 2. We then add the 10 to the 49 to get 59 and add 2 for a result of 61. Implicit in such assumptions are properties of the operations of multiplication and addition that students begin to investigate in elementary classrooms. When students explore such properties, they not only learn to make and justify generalizations, but they also come to understand more fully the computational strategies they use every day.

- Relationships between operations: Flexible and accurate computations often require that students move between different operations in the same problem. In this module, we will study, for example, how students work through the idea that addition and subtraction are systemically related operations—*any* problem that can be solved by finding a missing addend can also be solved by subtracting.

- Results of operating on particular kinds of numbers: In the vignette above, Myra and her classmates were studying what happens when you add even numbers. In this module, we will also examine operations on negative numbers, as well as the special case of 0. Many of the generalizations that are developed can easily be understood and justified if the numbers involved are the counting numbers (1, 2, 3,...). However, what happens if the number system is extended to include zero and negative numbers? Do all of the same generalizations still make sense? Are they still true? If so, why? For example, if we add 3 and $^{-}4$, does the order of addends matter? Does $3 + {}^{-}4$ yield the same result as ${}^{-}4 + 3$?

When students begin to state and justify such generalizations, they tend to use diagrams, concrete objects, and words to do so—just as Myra did in her statement about adding two even numbers. As their statements become more complicated, they begin to need other ways to point at "the first number," "the bigger number," "the answer you get when you add two numbers," and so forth. This is the beginning of what later becomes conventional algebraic notation. In this module, we look at the early stages of this process and consider when it is useful and productive for students to begin to make this shift.

The cases in this Casebook were written by elementary and middle-school teachers recounting episodes from their classrooms. The range represents schools in urban, suburban, and rural communities. The teacher-authors, who were themselves working to understand the "big ideas" of the elementary and middle-grade mathematics curriculum, wrote these cases as part of their own process of inquiry. They came together on a regular basis to read and discuss each other's developing work.

The K–5 teachers who participated in the program found that this work deepens students' understanding of arithmetic, the heart of their mathematics program. Middle-school teachers said that the work supported students' early study of algebra. In the words of one teacher, "By explicitly stating the generalizations and then finding examples, counterexamples, and proofs, students are thinking more about the principles that underlie their work. Generalizations help students see relationships among and between numbers, and among and between operations."

Teacher collaborators report that students who tend to have difficulty in mathematics become stronger mathematical thinkers through this work. As one teacher wrote, "When I began to work on generalizations with my students, I noticed a shift in my less capable learners. Things seemed more accessible to them." When the generalizations are made explicit—through language and through visual representation used to justify them—they become accessible to more students and can become the foundation for greater computational fluency. Furthermore, the disposition to create a representation when a mathematical question arises supports students in reasoning through their confusions.

At the same time, students who generally outperform their peers in mathematics find this content challenging and stimulating. The study of numbers and operations extends beyond efficient computation to the excitement of making and proving conjectures about mathematical relationships that apply to an infinite class of numbers. A teacher explained, "Students develop a habit of mind of looking beyond the activity to search for something more, some broader mathematical context to fit the experience into."

Through the cases, you will study students' initial ideas as they develop their algebraic thinking. We will look at students' arguments as they work to "prove" such generalizations as subtracting a smaller amount produces a larger result; switching around numbers in an addition or multiplication problem gives the same answer, but switching the numbers in a subtraction or division problem does not; a factor of a number is *always* also a factor of that number's multiples.

In the seminar sessions, you will have opportunities to work through these and related mathematical ideas for yourself. You will identify patterns in the number system, articulate the generalizations you see, and work to prove them. You will explore how the consistency of the number system determines calculations with negative numbers. In addition, you will look at how students' generalizations, and your own, appear when represented in algebraic notation.

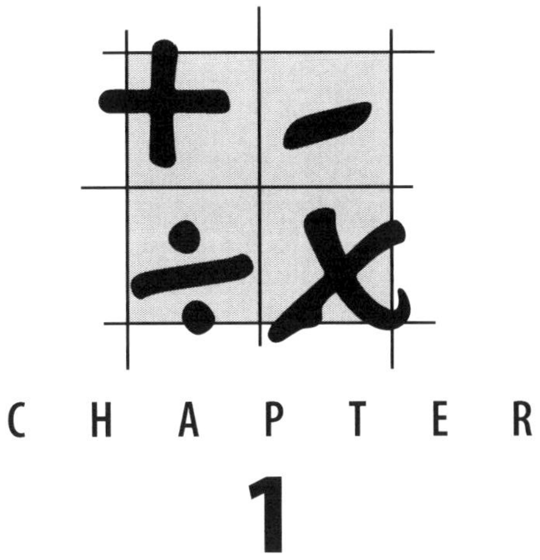

CHAPTER 1

Discovering Rules for Odds and Evens

CASE 1	Number of the day	Dolores	Grade 3, October
CASE 2	Reds are even; blacks are odd	Nadine	Grade 1, October
CASE 3	Why can't you count to 5 by 2s?	Ingrid	Grade 2, February
CASE 4	Adding evens	Lucy	Grade 3, June
CASE 5	Defining even numbers	Carl	Grades 7–9, September

One day, a second-grade student asked, "Why is it that you can count to 10 by 5s, and you can count to 10 by 2s, but you can't count to 5 by 2s?" Although he asked his question in terms of specific numbers, he might be wondering about a more general issue. A third grader in a different school was wondering about a similar question. Staring at the two rows of five cubes he had created by separating ten cubes, he said, "It's like what I've been wondering since like kindergarten. How does two odd numbers equal an even number?"

The behavior of odd and even numbers often piques the curiosity of students, young and old. Though their questions may arise from considering specific numbers, they are soon drawn to make generalizations about whole classes of numbers—for example, that any two odd numbers added together make an even number.

In the cases featured in this chapter, students in grades 1 through 9 are discussing odd and even numbers. As you read the cases, consider the following questions: Are students making generalizations? If so, what are they, and what makes them general? What do students do to convince themselves or their classmates as to the validity of the generalizations?

CASE 1

Number of the day

Dolores

GRADE 3, OCTOBER

I decided to open an exploration of odd and even numbers by asking my new class of third graders to share what they already knew. When I asked what they had learned earlier, one boy's hand shot up immediately. Then he struggled for a minute, searching for the wording he wanted, before saying, "I could say it to myself in my head, but I can't explain it now." Other students contributed comments on what they had learned:

CORY: Odd numbers are like one, that's the first one in the odd family.

EVA: Even numbers are 2, 4, 6, 8, and so on.

KIM: Even numbers in the ones place are usually the even numbers, so 2, 4, 6, 8, 0. You can test 32. Just pay attention to the 2. It's even.

DOUG: 9 is on my soccer shirt. It's odd. So is 1, 3, 5, 7, 9.

AMY: We can start with 1 and go maybe to 100; it goes odd, even, odd, even, odd. I think zero is even, too.

JACK: If zero is at the end of the number, it is even. So in 100, you look at the last zero for even. 100 is 50 and 50. 30 is 15 and 15. 50 is 25 and 25. 40 is 20 and 20.

MARGE: If zero is in a number, it doesn't make it even, does it? Like 101, the end matters right?

Dolores

GRADE 3, OCTOBER

As the discussion continued, it seemed most children, like Jack, were using the definition that an even number can be divided into two equal parts using only whole numbers. I discussed that definition with students before we went on. Then the class got busy trying to divide numbers that end with zero into two equal parts. This lasted for about 10 minutes and, after offering help to each other, the students determined that all of the numbers were "splittable."

Next, I asked students to try to find out what kind of a number we would get as an answer if we added an even number to an even number. They set off to try all sorts of possibilities. As we came back together at the end of the period, all 20 children reported that their sums were even, after a few addition corrections.

The next day, I reminded the class of the work we had completed earlier, emphasizing the definitions of even and odd numbers. Then I gave each child a sheet of paper with the question, How can we be sure an even number added to an even number will give an answer that is even? Students supplied a variety of responses:

RICKY: We will never know because there's too many numbers.

D. C.: We could never tell because the numbers don't stop.

LAURIE: We can never know for sure because the numbers do not stop.

EVA: We really can't! Because we might not know about an even number and if we add it with 2 it might equal an odd number!

ZOE: I know it will add to an even number because 4 + 4 = 8 and 8 + 8 = 16.

CLAUDIA: We don't know because numbers don't end. 1,000,000 + 100; you can always add another hundred.

MIM: Your answer will be even because you are using even numbers.

Building on this background of thinking about odd and even numbers, I decided to try something new based on the number of the day. As we make our way through 182 school days, I begin each day with "Happy Day #...." A usual activity is to think of interesting arithmetic expressions that equal the number of the day. We also figure out ways to determine the number of days ahead of us in the year.

I decided to ask the children to create problems that would have answers of 24, but this time they had to work with some restrictions.

Dolores

GRADE 3, OCTOBER

They could only use the operation of addition and only even numbers to get the sum.

My third graders threw themselves into this task. In just a few minutes, everyone had a supply of math sentences to share. For the most part, they were all done correctly. There were just a few arithmetic errors. Sometimes the difficulty was in keeping track of how many 2s were in the problem.

The next day, we worked on making problems with sums of 25 using the same restrictions. Again, the children busied themselves with calculations. After a few minutes of working alone, we talked about what they had found. A few kids raised their hands to offer ideas. In each case, an odd number had "snuck" into the equation. No one actually said they could not do it. The comments revealed more of a mood that they had not found a way to do it yet. Thinking back on this, I wish I had asked if 24 had been easier to do, and if so, why. I wish I had pushed a little on their thinking. I knew we would come back to this on another "odd" day.

I am often wondering about how and when children notice patterns. I knew it would take a few times at this same kind of work for third graders to expect particular results. This first time I think they were pretty focused on actually getting even numbers and adding correctly.

On day 28, we tried using only odd numbers to add up to 28. There were lots of 1 + 1 + 1 + 1 +.... For the most part the class had little difficulty with this. They just poured themselves into the job. The next day they breezed through finding odd numbers that totaled 29. No one noticed an odd number of odd numbers was needed to get an odd sum. They were happily and busily adding. (There will still be time to notice those patterns.)

As days passed I continued to work on making math time more than just doing calculations. It is always a lot of work at the beginning of a year to get a new batch of children to appreciate the value of sharing ideas with each other. There is such a tendency to just take turns talking without recognizing that they also need to consider the ideas and strategies of others.

I was also wondering if students were noticing trends, rules, and patterns with numbers by doing lots of examples. Could they help each other make generalizations?

The next time we did the "number of the day" work was on day 33. I gave the kids a few minutes to try to make the number 33 with the restrictions of using only addition and only even numbers. The results were interesting.

Dolores

GRADE 3, OCTOBER

Mim immediately wrote in giant-sized letters on the back of her spelling pretest, "YOU CAN'T DO IT!! evens 10 + 10 + 10 + 2 + 2 can't do it!! Sorry, you can't do it. "

Kim wrote, "16 + 16 = 32 There is no posiple way to make 33 with all even numbers. You can only make evens with all evens. "

Claudia said, "Even numbers plus even numbers always adds up to even, and 33 is odd."

Carry insisted, "You can't do it. You would at least use 1 odd. You can't make 33 with only even numbers."

Jack tested it out by adding a string of twos. He wrote, "2 + 2 + 2 + 2 + 2 + 2 + 2 + 2 + 2 + 2 + 2 + 2 + 2 + 2 + 2 + 2 + 2 – 1 = 33 I trid and I can't come up with even numbers to = 33."

Noah had lots of calculations on his page, which were crossed out. Below all of that he wrote, "You can't do it."

Beth used a different strategy. She put together a series of even numbers and ended up with sums of 32 or 34:

30 + 2 + 2 = 34
20 + 10 + 2 + 2 = 34
10 + 12 + 10 = 32
10+ 10 + 10 + 4 = 34

She didn't make any generalizations.

Anna did some exploring and made an observation:

1 + 4 + 4 + 2 + 10 + 10 + 2   1 is odd. I think it is not posable.
10 + 10 + 10 + 2 + 1 = 33   1 IS ODD.
10 + 10 + 10 + 2 = 32   You need one more but one is odd.

Eva tried something similar:

20 + 12 = 32 NO   30 + 2 + 1 ODD I think this problem can not be done with the even numbers we know.

Others took time to try but made no "discoveries" or generalizations. As we came together to talk about it, everyone was relieved to find it could not work. I think it is still a "number-specific" idea for about half of the children. I expect they will jump into trying many combinations of even numbers to make numbers 39 and 41, and maybe even 55. It may take time for them to get it.

CASE 2

Reds are even; blacks are odd

Nadine

GRADE 1, OCTOBER

One of our regular morning activities involves the number of days we have been in school. Instead of using a number line, we keep track of numbers in a 10 × 10 grid. (I will add a second grid on the 100th day of school.) Our chart starts with 0 and a new number is added every day, so on the first day 0 and 1 were filled in. The last number will be 180 for the last day of school. We alternate using red and black pens, so the even numbers are written in red and odds are written in black.

The discussion I am writing about was initiated by my students on day 19, so the chart looked like this:

0	1	2	3	4	5	6	7	8	9
10	11	12	13	14	15	16	17	18	19

The children wanted to tell one another what they noticed about the chart. I wrote down their observations.

- This is a pattern: red, black, red, black.
- There's a column of red—0, 10—and then a column of black—1, 11—and then a column of red—2, 12—and then black—3, 13—and it keeps going. (Anita had said "rows," but I pointed out that because they were going up and down, we call them "columns.")
- There is a 0 in the first box, and then there's a 1 with a 0 for the ten in the box under it.
- The same thing happens with the other numbers. The number on the top row shows up right under it with a one in front of it.
- The red numbers are even; the black ones are odd.

Nadine

GRADE 1, OCTOBER

We had never talked about odd and even numbers before, so I asked, "What is even? What is odd?"

Some students called out numbers: "4 is even." "3 is odd." I decided that today, I would just listen, and based on what I heard, would work to design a lesson later.

Terry noticed that half the numbers were red—0, 2, 4, 6, 8, 10, 12, 14, 16, 18 (10 numbers)—and half were black—1, 3, 5, 7, 9, 11, 13, 15, 17, 19 (10 numbers).

Jack said that the next number, 20, would be even. He knew that because of two things: 1) it would be red, and 2) 10 + 10 = 20. He continued his explanation: "If you take two numbers that are even and put them together, you have an even number." I was extremely impressed. He then added, "You *have to* have two even numbers to make another even number."

The students now had cubes out so Jack could show everyone else what he meant. He showed us two stacks of 10; then he put them together to make 20.

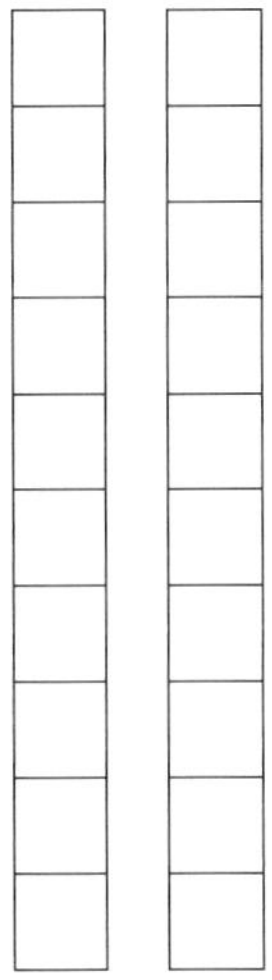

Shay, listening very carefully to Jack, added, "What about 3 + 3?" Shay held up two stacks of 3 cubes. "The 3s are odd, but when you put them together, it makes 6, and 6 is even."

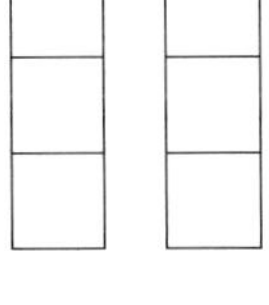

Nadine

GRADE 1, OCTOBER

Jack looked back at his recorded statement that you have to have two even numbers to make another even number and said, "I can fix that. If you take two numbers that are the same and put them together, it makes an even number."

At this point, the discussion was very interesting for several of my students, but I was definitely losing the attention of the rest of the class. So we stopped there. I have plenty to think about. What made my day was Jack's comment just before lunch: "Math discussions are really fun."

CASE 3

Why can't you count to 5 by 2s?

Ingrid

GRADE 2, FEBRUARY

One day, at the end of a recent math activity, Sam said he had a question. "Why is it that you can count to 10 by 5s, and you can count to 10 by 2s, but you can't count to 5 by 2s?" I told Sam that his question was too important to try to think about in the time we had left, but promised we would return to it the next day. I could not have come up with a better question to get at what my students might be thinking about odd and even numbers and how they relate to each other.

The following day, I asked my students to be prepared to use cubes to explore Sam's question and then demonstrate their thinking to the class.

CALVIN: Me and Craig were thinking of taking 5 cubes.... If you have 5 cubes and you break them up into 2s, you have 1 missing. So, it's 2, 4, and not 6, it's 5 because there's two 2s that makes 4 and there's 1 more after the 2s to make 5.

GRADE 2, FEBRUARY

Calvin points to this model.

TEACHER: Could somebody say in his or her own words what Calvin and Craig were noticing?

JEREMY: I don't get it, because if you put another 1 onto the 5, it will equal 6, not 5.

CALVIN: If I put 1 to that 1, it would equal 6, and I'm not doing that. I'm counting to 5 on 2s and I was doing 4 here with two even numbers. (Calvin again points to his model.) 2 and 2 are even numbers. 1 is an odd number and if we have three even numbers, that would make 6 to make another even number, but we're trying to make an odd number and it's 5 and it's very difficult to understand, because... I just don't know what to say.

It appears that Calvin is interjecting some thoughts about odd and even numbers that he has accumulated on his way to second grade. I am concerned that the conversation will head off into recalling notions about "odds" and "evens" and stray away from Sam's question, so I decide to set aside the general ideas of odds and evens for now. I make an attempt at refocusing the conversation to stick specifically to the numbers Sam asked about.

TEACHER: I'm hearing words like *odd* and *even*. We don't have to use those words. What I think I hear Calvin saying is, "If you put another cube down, you would have 6, but we can only have 5 cubes. So you can't get there by 2s. You can only get to 4, and the next number would be 6. When you have 5 cubes, you have two groups of two and one cube left over."

CALVIN: Yes, to make 5.

TEACHER: The next part of Sam's question is, "You can't count to 5 by 2s, but you can count to 10 by 2s and 5s. What's happening there?"

CALVIN: Craig got this idea, so I think that he should explain it.

Craig has been a silent partner up to this point. He does not like to be the spokesperson, but he uses the following model to help his classmates understand:

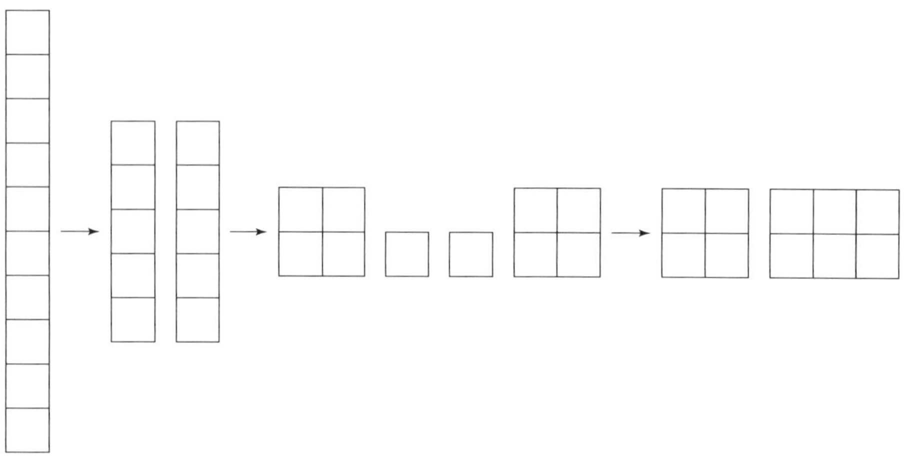

Sam says that Craig has not answered his question. I'm not sure that most of the class understands what Craig has done, so I ask for a paraphrase. Janelle is happy to oblige.

JANELLE: He took 10 cubes, and he took 5 off of them, and then he put 2 in a block of cubes and another 2 in a block of cubes, and then 1 was left. And then he did the same with the other 5. And then the two 1s that were left he put together, and that made another 2 and that made it equal 10.

Calvin feels the need to point out a difference between Janelle's explanation and Craig's model. In Craig's model, the leftover from one group of 5 is added to the other group to make a group of 6.

CALVIN: Craig is saying that, if you have the 4 and the 1, the 2 and the 2 and the 1; he made a copy of it over here. Then he saw these two loose ones that were not together, and he took this one and put it with the other group, and then he made 6 and 4. And that is how you make 10 by 2s, but it's actually by 5s a little, too.

GRADE 2, FEBRUARY

I wonder if Craig's model might obscure the idea that each group of five has one left over, which comes through in Janelle's explanation. So I decide to model what she has said.

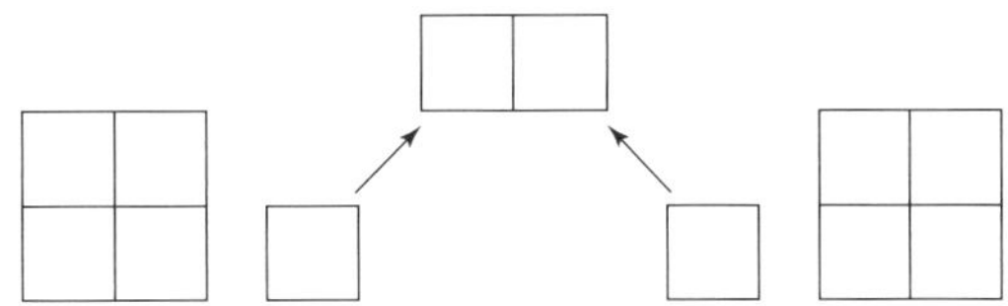

TEACHER: So Craig had two groups of 5 and each of those groups of 5 had one left over. He moved the extra from one group and put it with the other group. What if I took the extra 1 from one group of 5 and put it with the extra 1 from the other group of 5? Does that show it in a different way?

CALVIN: It would be the same thing as Craig did, but these are separated from the two 4s. If you add those 2 to one of these 4s, then it would be 6. It would be 6 + 4 and that would be easier to think about.

TEACHER: Which would be easier to think about?

CALVIN: Now that you took the two up there, now no one will get confused by the way Craig does it.

TEACHER: So that feels clearer to you, to take the extra 1s and put them together.

SAM: I have another idea. What Craig and Calvin did, that gave me an idea.

Sam splits the two cubes apart and returns one cube to each of the sets of 4 cubes.

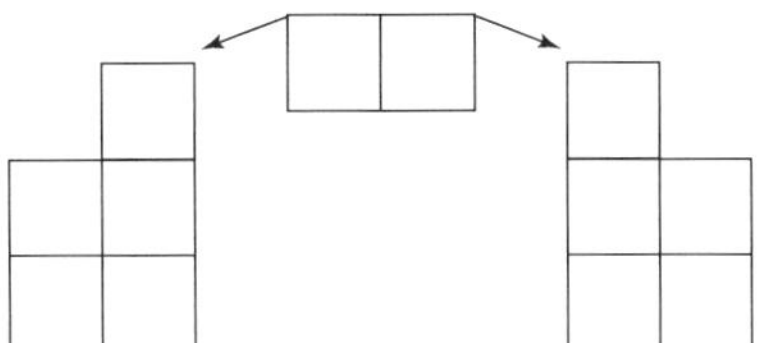

Then he picks up the two sets of 5 and joins them together to make columns of 5 cubes.

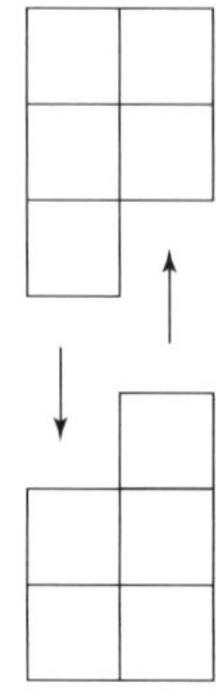

SAM: That equals 10. If you take them apart, they equal 5,
and that makes 5 an odd number. This equals 10—2, 4, 355
6, 8, 10.

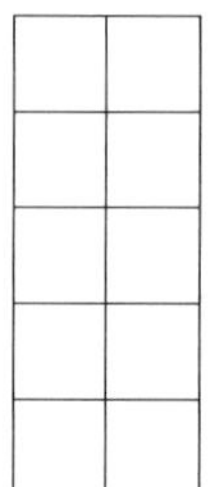

SAM: And this equals 5.

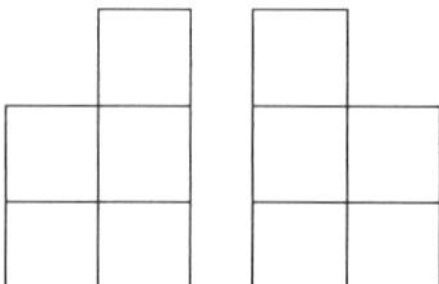

TEACHER: So, it looks like you're showing the extra ls on each 5 coming together to make a pair.

CASE 4

Adding evens

GRADE 3, JUNE

I set out to investigate odd and even numbers with my class. As third graders, they had worked on odd and even numbers before, but to make sure we were all on the same page, we started our session with a discussion about how to define these terms. We agreed that even numbers are those that can be made into pairs with none left over, or that they can be divided into two equal groups with none left over. (We did clarify that those groups needed to be whole numbers—not fractions.) Some of the children pointed out that even numbers are numbers you get to when you count by 2, starting with 2. We also agreed that if you have a number that fits one of those conditions—it can be made into pairs, it can be made into two equal groups, or it can be reached by counting by 2—it also fits the other conditions.

The class defined odd numbers as those that have one left over when you make pairs or when you try to make two equal groups.

Next, I gave the class a worksheet I had created. I intended to have students practice applying these definitions. I didn't want them just to say whether a number is odd or even but to show how they used the definition to make this determination. Then, I wanted them to see if they could predict whether sums of given pairs of numbers are even or odd. The questions on the worksheet were:

1. Are these numbers odd or even? How do you know? What rules or pictures can you write to show your thinking about whether a number is odd or even?

    6
    9
    35
    92

Lucy

GRADE 3, JUNE

2. Are the answers to these problems odd or even? Do you know without solving them? Why is that? Show your thinking with pictures or explain with words.
   $4 + 8 =$
   $5 + 3 =$
   $4 + 5 =$
   $9 + 2 =$
3. Does your thinking work for these problems, too? Why? Do you know if the answer is odd or even without solving the problem? How do you know?
   $35 + 49 =$
   $66 + 105 =$
   $96 + 244 =$
4. Do your rules work for any size numbers? Why is that?
5. How could you tell whether an answer was even or odd if you had more than two numbers?

When it was time to bring the class together for a whole-group discussion about what they had figured out from this activity, many students suggested generalizations—the sum of two evens is even; the sum of two odds is even—but none offered a proof. That is, nobody offered a proof until Amanda spoke up:

AMANDA: Two evens, no matter what they are, have to equal an even.

TEACHER: Why?

AMANDA: Um. I just figured out something.... If you counted something by 2s, and 2s always work on an even number, they can't work on an odd number, and every even number you count by 2s with it and if you added the 2s of both even numbers on top of each other, they both count by 2s, so they would have to equal an even.

At this point, I wasn't at all sure what Amanda was saying, but I wanted to give her classmates a chance to think together with her.

TEACHER: Does somebody know what Amanda is talking about? Ellen?

ELLEN: She's kind of talking about—No, I'm confused.

TEACHER: Does somebody want to hear it again? Ellen wants to hear it again, Amanda.

GRADE 3, JUNE

AMANDA: Well, if you have two even numbers, 2s work on both of them, so if you put them on top of each other. Umm. Can I have some cubes?

As Amanda built two sticks of cubes representing even numbers, she explained her idea again, showing the two sticks of cubes that could be counted by 2s, and then joining them to make one stick.

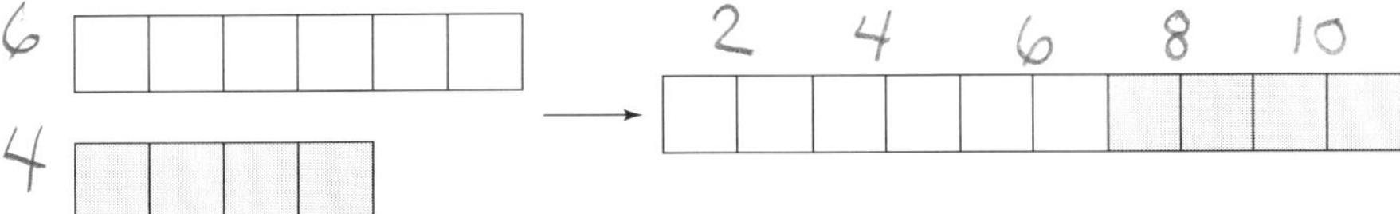

AMANDA: I have this, both of them (the two sticks) count by 2s, so if I put them on top of each other, you keep counting by 2s, and then you get to an even number.

Once I saw Amanda's demonstration with cubes, I understood what she was talking about.

TEACHER: Ohhhh. That's not what I thought you meant when you said you put them on top of each other. Ohh. What do people think about what Amanda just said? Elizabeth?

ELIZABETH: I think she said that if you have two even numbers, and they're counting by 2s, then you put them on top of each other.

TEACHER: You stick them together, I think that's what she meant.

ELIZABETH: Yeah. But then I don't know what she said after that.

TEACHER: (Checking with Amanda to make sure she's correctly paraphrasing) So, you've got an even number over here, and an even number over here, and you stick them together. Doing that has to give you an even number.

AMANDA: Because you can count by 2s up to 6 and if I add the 4 on, you can just keep counting up by 2s, and that would have to equal an even number because 2s only get you to even numbers.

At this point, Elizabeth was working hard to follow Amanda's proof. At first, she seemed to agree that the generalization felt right. Then she reconsidered.

Elizabeth: I think she's just like adding the even numbers that are counting by 2s, so if she had two even numbers on both sides and then put them together, then she would get an even number, so it's kind of like you're adding the even numbers.

Teacher: But why would it be an even number, if she had an even number and another even and she put them together. Why do you...does it feel like she's right, that it has to be an even?

Elizabeth: Well, yes... Well, I don't know, because in some cases, well, um, I can't really think of it now but like, if you had one that was an even plus an even, if like, I haven't figured this out, but sometime maybe it could equal an odd.

Teacher: And Amanda's saying it couldn't ever equal odd. Is that what you're saying, Amanda? That an even plus an even could never equal odd? And Elizabeth is wondering if it (the sum) sometimes could be an odd, but you're saying it could never be an odd? Do you want to say more about why that is?

Amanda: Because 2s don't get to odds. And if they're two even numbers, they're both counting by 2s, and if you put them on top of each other you keep counting by 2s and that always equals an even number.

Elizabeth: So she's saying she already knows that it always equals it.

Teacher: Amanda thinks she knows that it's always going to be even.

That is as far as we got today, but it leaves me with much to think about. Amanda has come up with what seems to be a very convincing proof, based on counting by 2s, that the sum of two even numbers must always be even. Elizabeth seemed quite close to understanding Amanda's argument, but she just doesn't seem able to make a claim about *all* even numbers. "I can't really think of it now, but...sometime maybe it could equal an odd," she said. Certainly, these two girls are in two different places with regard to thinking about and proving generalizations.

But should I think of Elizabeth's position as weak for a third grader? No. Actually grasping the notion that numbers go on forever is new for children at this age. It is important that Elizabeth realizes it is not sufficient to argue that a generalization is always true simply by looking at particular examples. After all, the examples chosen might be special cases, and something might change with other numbers. Elizabeth's insight is key toward understanding the need for mathematical proof based on *reasoning*, rather than *by example*.

Elizabeth and Amanda's classmates were quiet during their exchange. I don't know where they are with these ideas, and this is something for me to look into in coming days.

CASE 5

Defining even numbers

Carl

GRADES 7–9, SEPTEMBER

As I begin the school year, I see a focus on odd and even numbers as an opportunity to convey something about the heart of mathematical endeavor: that it is about ideas and reasoning; that it is about looking for patterns, making claims, and trying to show why those claims are true. I also want to illustrate the power of using different representations when considering mathematical ideas and situations.

Representations organize information and enhance our perception of features and relationships that might not be obvious upon first consideration. It is often through contrasts between different representations that these features and relationships become apparent. These new perceptions are powerful tools for reasoning about the situation. I want students to value and develop skill using representations so that they see the use of diagrams, physical models, graphs, stories, and verbal arguments is as essential to doing mathematics as the ability to compute or solve equations. Finally, I hope to encourage the development of a learning community in which students view themselves and classmates as partners in making sense of mathematics and their world. I want them to learn to listen to their own ideas and the ideas of their classmates. I want them to feel comfortable sharing their ideas with others and using the ideas of others to help them make mathematical progress.

Carl

GRADES 7–9, SEPTEMBER

It was with these goals in mind that I started the session about odd and even numbers. I put the following prompt on the board: "What is an even number? How do you know?" I instructed students to write their ideas in their journal. After a couple of minutes, I had students share what they had written with their "Think Team" (groups of three). After a couple more minutes, we had the following class discussion:

Teacher: So, let's hear some of your ideas.

Alexander: It is any number that ends in 0, 2, 4, 6, or 8.

I expect that most of my students came in with this characterization of even numbers, but I wanted to go beyond that, to think about the importance of 2 in the structure of even numbers. This would be necessary for the goals that I had for the next session in which we would be making arguments about sums of odd and even numbers. So, I pushed the class on Alexander's idea.

Teacher: How do you know that? How do you know that is true for all numbers, even really big ones?

David: It is just the way even numbers are.

Teacher: So what about 90? It ends in zero but 9 is odd, so I think 90 is odd.

The class buzzed with discussion, and after a few seconds I posed my question again.

Teacher: How are you going to convince me that 90 is even?

Krista: The 9 is not a "9," but it means nine 10s.

Teacher: So how is that supposed to convince me?

Krista: We know 10 is even. Every one of the nine 10s is even, so 90 has to be even.

Teacher: This takes us back to the original question: "How do you know 10 is even?"

Kimberly: An even number is a number that you can divide by 2.

Chris: But I can divide 5 by 2 and 5 is not an even number.

Krista: I meant that it divides without leaving a remainder.

Vinod: You get a whole number when you divide by 2.

Carl

GRADES 7–9, SEPTEMBER

Now we were getting to a definition we could work with. I wrote on the board, "An even number is a number that can be divided by 2 with the result being a whole number."

WILLIAM: I have a different way. I was drawing cubes. I drew 6 using cubes and I saw that an even number is made up of pairs.

TEACHER: Let's have you come up here and draw it. Explain what you are seeing. I am going to ask someone else to restate what William is saying.

William drew the following:

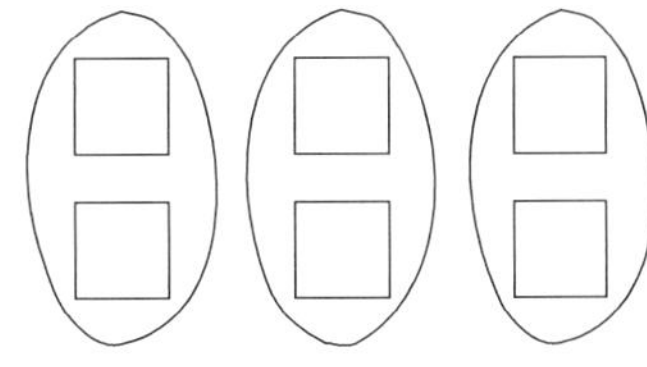

WILLIAM: I tried this a couple of times, and it always works.

TEACHER: So what do the rest of you think of this?

CAROLINA: It's like what I was thinking. An even number is a multiple of 2.

TEACHER: What do you mean by a multiple of 2?

CAROLINA: It is something that is made up of 2s.

BRIANNA: Two times 4. It's multiplication. Eight is 2 times 4.

TEACHER: What does that have to do with William's idea of pairs?

BRIANNA: There are pairs of 2 in 8...4 of them.

TEACHER: Interesting. So, it seems like we have two different ideas going on here.

The board now looked like this:

1. An even number is a number that can be divided by 2 with the result being a whole number.
2. An even number is a number that can be made up of pairs or multiples of 2.

Carl

GRADES 7–9, SEPTEMBER

TEACHER: How is it that we can have two different definitions for the same thing? Or do they define the same thing? I want you to talk in your Think Teams about these two ideas and decide if they are both true and why?

I watched students in their teams putting cubes together and breaking them in half or into pairs. After a few minutes, I called them back together.

TEACHER: Alex, I heard your group talking about something interesting. What were the three of you focusing on?

ALEX: We think both are true because they are kind of saying the same thing.

TEACHER: Explain what you mean.

ALEX: Any number that is made up of 2s has to be able to be divided by 2.

ALANA: It's like division. Multiplication is division backwards. Two times 4 is 8. Eight divided by 2 is 4.

KEVIN: I think I know why what we have been talking about is true for all even numbers. It's kind of like a chain of 2s.

TEACHER: (At first, I was not sure what he was meaning.) Kevin, before you explain your chain idea, help us get clear about what you are referring to. What are you thinking is true for even numbers?

KEVIN: Well, all of it...that all evens are made up of 2s and that all evens end in 0, 2, 4, 6, or 8. It's like a chain. Between zero and 2 is 1. Between 2 and 4 is 3. To get from 2 to 4 you have to add 2. There is no way to get from the number 2 to an odd number going by 2s. So if you keep adding 2s, the number has to be made up of 2s.

I wrote on the board:

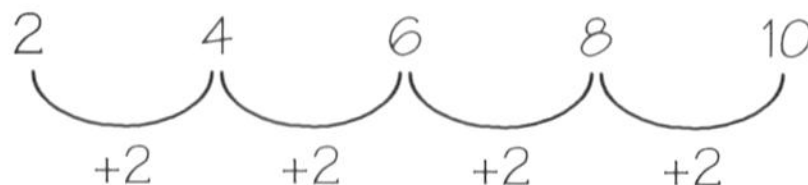

TEACHER: So, does this show what you are thinking?

KEVIN: Yes.

I asked the class to discuss Kevin's idea in their Think Teams, and then brought them back together again.

TEACHER: Zach, a few minutes ago you said something to your team. Before we see what everyone thinks about Kevin's "chain" argument, I would like you to say it to the whole group.

ZACH: You can't know something is true for all even numbers because there are too many.

BRIANNA: We talked about that, too. You can't ever convince someone because they can always think of other numbers we haven't tried.

TEACHER: Exactly. I wanted Zach to state this because it highlights something very important about mathematics. By looking at many examples, we can never be totally confident that something is true because there are more numbers than we can try. But with mathematics we can think about the structure of the situation; we can think about what is happening with the numbers and come up with an argument based on that structure to explain why. This is why mathematics is so powerful and why I said that this class was going to be about developing your mathematical power to explain things that would be difficult to figure out otherwise. So, Kevin is noticing something about even numbers that he thinks explains why they always are made up of 2s and why they always end in 0, 2, 4, 6, or 8. Does anyone think they know what he is saying?

ELLA: Because numbers go odd-even-odd-even, you can never get to the number in between using 2s. You can get to a 1, 3, 5 by 2 or 2, 4, 6, but you can't get between these.

TEACHER: So, because evens have this "every other" quality, the idea of 2s is built into them.

TAYLOR: Mr. Fromm, but what about four point four? Isn't that even?

This statement surprised me. I needed to know what she was thinking. I didn't just want to say no because she may have a very powerful rationale for why she thinks that 4.4 is even. I do not want to undermine her sense of being able to make sense of the math. I am also aware that one other group was talking about 5.3 as being odd.

TEACHER: What leads you to believe that 4.4 is even?

TAYLOR: Four is even and 4.4 can be divided by 2.

TEACHER: I like the way you are thinking about this and trying to make sense of the ideas. This is exactly how a mathematician might think: Are there any cases that seem to contradict what we are thinking? First of all, 4 is, of course, even but what does "point 4" mean?

TAYLOR: It means four tenths.

TEACHER: Yes. So this is like what you were saying about the number 90 earlier. The 9 is odd, but the 9 in 90 means 9 tens.

TAYLOR: Oh, yeah. The .4 is not really a 4 but four tenths.

Taylor's question now became an opportunity for the class. I asked students to create an argument to explain why they think 4.4 is or is not even. After a few minutes, I brought them back together.

ALEX: We say it is not because when you divide by 2 you get 2.2. This is not a whole number.

MARGOT: We don't think it is even because you can't make 4.4 with 2s. Two plus 2 is 4, and 2 plus 2 plus 2 is 6. You can't get to 4.4.

TEACHER: Wow, you have been doing some powerful thinking. You can see that our Think Teams are working. We are helping each other to make sense of stuff, and we are using each other's ideas to come up with new insights into evens. Taylor's question forced us to really think harder and to apply what we have been talking about. Way to go. I can't wait for tomorrow. Before we end this session, I have one more thing for you to think about.

Carl

GRADES 7–9, SEPTEMBER

I wrote on the board:

> Based on the work we have been doing with even numbers, write a definition for odd numbers.

I feel very pleased about this discussion because I think that, as a class, we were able to make some progress toward my goals. At the same time, I am wondering where each student is in his or her thinking about these ideas. I am going to need to look closely at each student's homework. I am also concerned about Danny. I noticed that Danny had written on his paper that an odd number is a strange or weird number. Is he thinking about the everyday sense of the term *odd*? Does he notice the "one left over" feature of odd numbers? I will need to pay attention to his ideas about adding odds tomorrow.

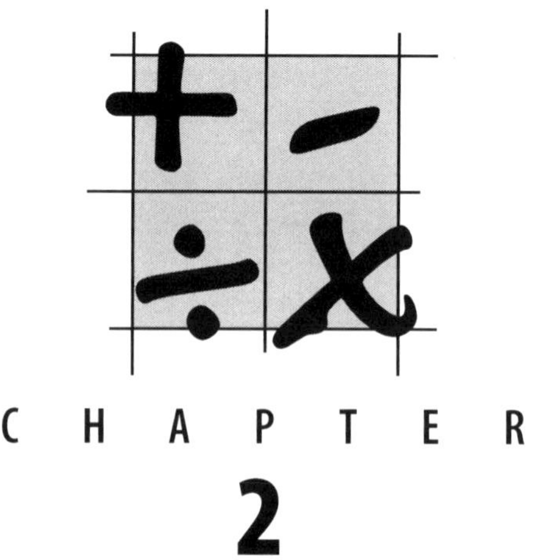

CHAPTER 2

Finding Relationships in Addition and Subtraction

CASE 6	Double compare	Lola	Kindergarten, April
CASE 7	Adding 1 to an addend	Maureen	Grade 2, June
CASE 8	Was it something I said?	Kate	Grade 2, February
CASE 9	Is it two more or two less?	Monica	Grade 4, November
CASE 10	$37 + 16 = 40 + x$	Carl	Grade 7, January

In the first two Number and Operations modules of DMI, *Building a System of Tens* and *Making Meaning for Operations*, we saw how students devise strategies for computation. Frequently, the strategy involves first solving an easier, related problem and then, if necessary, adapting the answer. Implicit in such computational methods are generalizations about numerical relationships with the operation being used. In this chapter, students are in the midst of their work on adding and subtracting, but here they pause, often with the encouragement of their teacher, to articulate the generalization that underlies their strategy.

Students also consider the question, Why does this strategy work? To understand why a generalization holds, it is often helpful to use a representation that embodies the operation and can be generalized to all numbers (or, at least, to all numbers currently under consideration).

As you read the cases, articulate for yourself the generalizations students are working on. Write out your generalizations in common language and in symbolic language.

CASE 6

Double compare

Lola

KINDERGARTEN, APRIL

This afternoon when I was working with part of my class, the children begged to be allowed to play Compare for math time. Compare is a card game very similar to War. I thought, Why not? but decided that I would introduce Double Compare as an option as well. In Double Compare, each player lays down the top two number cards from his or her pile. The player with the higher total when the numbers on the cards are combined says "me." The numerals on the cards are zero through six, and each card has little pictures of objects to show the quantity represented.

I put the students into pairs, and they went off to play. Three pairs played Double Compare, and one played Compare as I circulated around the room.

As I watched, a situation came up with several groups: Each player would have one card equal to one of the partner's cards and one card that was different. When Martina had 6 and 2 and Karen had 6 and 1, Karen quickly said "You." I asked how she knew and she pointed to the 2 and said, "This is big. Even though these are the same (the 6s), this (the 6 and 2) must be more."

Paul and his partner had a very similar set of hands. Paul put down 6 and 3 and his partner put down 6 and 1. Paul said, "I had 6, and he had 6, and then I had a higher number." I asked what their cards added up to, and both of them counted the pictures on their cards to find the totals.

Lola

KINDERGARTEN, APRIL

As they continued to play, they did not count to figure out totals or who had more but did accurately figure out who got to say "me." On a turn a minute later, Paul had 4 and 3, and his partner had 4 and 5. Paul's comment was, "I have 3 and he has 5." He knew he could basically ignore the two 4s.

In another hand that I observed, Karen had 6 and 5, and Martina had 0 and 2. Karen said "Me, because she got two low numbers."

After a while, I realized that it seemed almost no one was adding or counting to figure out totals. I looked around some more, mostly just collecting data mentally about whether I saw adding, counting, or discussion of totals. I saw just a tiny bit.

It was time to clean up and meet on the rug. Once we were all settled, we discussed how students knew who got to say "me." We talked for a while about how the students "ignored" cards when each partner had the same one and only paid attention to the cards that were different. Martina said that 6 and 3 is more than 6 and 1 because 3 is bigger than 1. I asked, "What about the 6s?" and she said, "They're the same." Paul added, "They don't matter. You don't have to pay attention to the 6s." I pointed out to them that when I put down 6 and 1, they said, "That's 7," but when I put down 6 and 3, no one figured out the sum. "Would 6 and 3 make a higher number than 6 and 1?" I heard 8! 9! 10! They settled on 9 by counting the pictures and because Danielle said 6 plus 3 is 9. "Is 9 more than 7?" Yes!

These students seem to have made a generalization; that a number added to a larger number is greater than the same number added to a smaller number. I put out a few more sets of cards, varying the number that was the same. "Does this only work for 6?" "No." They said it always works, and Paul reiterated that you don't have to pay attention to the numbers that are the same.

Another generalization most of them seemed to recognize was that the sum of two smaller numbers is less than the sum of two larger numbers. Karen's comment that she got two low numbers expressed this idea. I asked the group about this. I put out 1 and 5 and 0 and 4, which had been a hand in Amanda and Danielle's game. I asked how Amanda knew she had more. She said, "This (5) is bigger than this (4), and this (1) is bigger than this (0)." I asked if it would work with other numbers, and everyone said, "Yes." We worked on more examples, and they were all saying it worked. Students were not adding and counting. They were "just knowing."

Lola

KINDERGARTEN, APRIL

Implicit in the children's actions were two generalizations. The children were close to articulating the first generalization: "You don't have to pay attention to the 6s." I wonder what it will take for them to have words for their second generalization beyond simply saying they "just knew."

CASE 7

Adding 1 to an addend

Maureen

GRADE 2, JUNE

I decided to investigate my students' thinking concerning what happens when you add one more to an addend, resulting in an answer that increases by one. I hope to explore these questions: What do my students understand? What do they understand beyond seeing a pattern of adding 1 more to an addend and the answer "going one higher"? How will they explain it? Will they begin to generalize their idea to include other numbers or all numbers?

I recorded the lesson. The following episode includes the highlights of our discussion.

I begin the lesson using some simple doubles. I ask students to pretend they are explaining to a first grader, who doesn't understand, what happens to the numbers when you add one more to one of the addends. I write on the board:

$4 + 4 = 8 \qquad 4 + 5 = 9$

Tia begins. She came to our school late in the year and is just beginning to feel comfortable talking about her ideas in math class. Looking at the double $4 + 4 = 8$, she explains that the answer is 8 because she counted up from 4 on her fingers. She demonstrates. This is something she has been working on the past few weeks. Some students continue the discussion.

Maureen

GRADE 2, JUNE

ESTER: If you have 4 + 4 = 8, right? You're adding 1 to the other 4. It gets you to 5. So that's 4 + 5 = 9. (Ester gets cubes to demonstrate.)

TEACHER: What changed in the number sentence? (Referring to the number sentences on the chart board: 4 + 4 = 8, 4 + 5 = 9.)

CONNIE: The 4 changed to a 5. The number always changes. You are just adding one more to the 4.

TEACHER: So did anything else change in these equations?

TIA: You can see a pattern. I see the 8, and I see the 9 and the 4 and the 5.

TEACHER: How come the 8 changed to a 9, Tia?

TIA: If you add 4 and the other 4, you get the answer 8. I see the 8 changed into a 9.

TEACHER: Why did the 8 change to a 9?

TIA: Cause 4 + 5 = 9.

TERRY: Because the 4 and 4; the last 4 gives 1 to the 5 and makes 9.

SEMA: (Gets cubes) You have 4 + 4 = 8. If you add 1 more to one of the 4s it equals 9. So, 5 + 4 = 9.

TEACHER: Anyone else?

CONNIE: If you... Sema says 5 + 4 = 9. They are just adding 1 more and putting it on the 4 so it can turn to a 5.

TEACHER: What else changed besides the 5?

CONNIE: The 8. The 8 changed to a 9.

TEACHER: Why did the 8 change to a 9?

ESTER: Because if you got the 4 and the 4, right? The—well you're adding one more to the other 4. It gives you 5. So that means that 8 changes to a 9.

TEACHER: Let's try something else. First graders might know 5 + 5 = 10. So, what would happen if we changed the number sentence to 5 + 6?

Maureen

GRADE 2, JUNE

TERRY: It equals 11 because the 5 from 5 + 5 = 10, it changed into a 6. It gives the other 5 a 1, and it changes into a 6 + 5 = 11.

TEACHER: I'm going to make the numbers a little bigger now. 21 + 23.

JOE: 44

TEACHER: What if I change it to 21 + 24? What would happen to the answer?

JOE: 45

TEACHER: Pretend that you're explaining to a first grader how the number sentence changes from 21 + 23 = 44 to 21 + 24 = 45.

JOE: The... (Long pause)

I repeat the question.

JOE: Because the 21 stayed the same, and 23 went higher, and the answer changed.

TEACHER: How much did the answer change by?

JOE: One.

TEACHER: Why did it change by 1?

JOE: Because you just add 1 to the 23.

TEACHER: Could I do it for other numbers?

CLASS: Yes.

TEACHER: If I did that with another number, what would happen?

SEMA: It would go to the next number. You add just 1 more, but if you were adding 2 more, it would go to the number after that one.

TEACHER: Can you think of another number sentence?

CONNIE: 51 + 53 equals... (Thinking it out, she whispers 50 + 50.)

JOE: (To Connie) What's 50 + 50?

CONNIE: 103

TEACHER: You're close.

Maureen

GRADE 2, JUNE

CONNIE: 104. I know that 50 + 50 = 100. I forgot to add the other one on the 3.

TEACHER: What would your next number sentence be?

CONNIE: 51 + 54 = 105

TEACHER: You didn't do much thinking about that. I didn't see you add the numbers.

CONNIE: The 53 changes to 1 more, 54, and you just add 1 more, so it's 105—because if you know the first one, you know the second one if you add 1 more.

TEACHER: Where did you add 1 more?

CONNIE: From the 104. I add the 1 more from the 104.

ESTER: Connie did not add from the 104. She added 1 more to the 53 to get to 105. She ended up on 54, and she got 105.

TEACHER: This is the big question. Ester says you didn't add the 1 to the 104. You added it to the 53 to make it 54. Can anyone talk about that? Where did we add the extra 1 and what happened?

CONNIE: I agree with Ester. You just added 53 and 1 more to make it a 54.

TEACHER: When we did that, what happened?

CONNIE: It equals 105.

ESTER: The answer changed to 105.

TERRY: (Looking at the list of numbers) First, you do it with doubles; then, you don't do it with doubles.

TEACHER: Does it work when I don't do it with doubles?

JOE: Yes.

TEACHER: How come?

JOE: Because it could work with any number.

TEACHER: Why?

CONNIE: It can work with any number because for the one I worked on, it did. You can do anything with the numbers.

Maureen

GRADE 2, JUNE

TEACHER: This is a tough question. I think some of you have answered it.

ESTER: You know how people say numbers never stop, so if you can do it with all these numbers, you can do it with the rest of the numbers, cause the numbers never stop, so if the numbers never stop, then you can do it with any kind of number you want. (I'm glad I had a tape recorder to follow this idea!)

JOE: It can work with any number because if it works with $0 + 1 = 1$; $0 + 2 = 2$.

TEACHER: What does that tell you?

JOE: It will work with any number.

SEMA: You're just adding 1 more to the other number. You'll make the next number after that one.

GIOVANNI: (Hesitantly offers an equation he's not sure will work) $10 + 0 = 10$; $10 + 1 = 11$.

TEACHER: Did the pattern work?

GIOVANNI: Yes.

At this point, students begin to consider larger numbers.

JOE: $1{,}000 + 10 = 1{,}010$; $1{,}000 + 11 = 1{,}011$.

TEACHER: Does the pattern work?

JOE: I don't know. It works with big and small numbers. It's a hard question.

As we take a break, some students "corner me" because they have more ideas that they would like to mention.

JOE: $50{,}000 + 1 = 50{,}001$; $50{,}000 + 2 = 50{,}002$.

ESTER and CONNIE: What about times (multiplication)? What about subtraction?

JOE: Adding one more to the number you had...to any number you pick, it changes 1 higher than the other one, than the other number. $10 + 10$. $10 + 11$. The 10 changes 1 higher.

Maureen

GRADE 2, JUNE

TEACHER: What else changes?

JOE: The answer.

I am surprised and impressed by how long these second-grade students "stayed" with this lesson, thinking hard and listening carefully to their classmates' ideas. They seemed to enjoy the give-and-take of the discussion.

In this lesson, students began to consider a wider variety of numbers than in previous lessons. I feel some students were seeking a different and new way to "prove" their conjecture.

In reviewing the lesson, I notice a "progression of ideas." I started the lesson by presenting smaller doubles 4 + 4 = 8 and 4 + 5 = 9. Soon, the students began to explore other possibilities: non-doubles. Connie introduced her own examples of 51 + 53 and 51 + 54. Joe wondered what would happen if 0 was one of the addends. This seemed like a different situation to him, but he worked through it. Next, the class tried bigger numbers 1,000 + 10; 1,000 + 11; 50,000 + 1; 50,000 + 2. As the lesson was winding down, Connie and Ester wondered, "What about times and subtraction?" As the tape ran out, Joe made what I consider a clear generalization, "Adding one more to the number you had—to any number you pick—it changes one higher than the other one, than the other number: 10 + 10 and 10 + 11. The 10 changes one higher." I questioned Joe, "What else changes?" Joe responded, "The answer."

CASE 8

Was it something I said?

Kate

GRADE 2, FEBRUARY

For the past year and a half, I have been involved in a teacher enhancement project in which we are examining the algebraic thinking of elementary school children. For me, this work has raised a lot of questions about the meaning and purpose of asking students to think algebraically.

Kate

GRADE 2, FEBRUARY

Last year, I spent a lot of time talking with my students about patterns that they would use to write a group of expressions that all equaled the same number. For example, if they needed to write expressions equal to 7, children would write 7 – 0 = 7; 8 – 1 = 7; 9 – 2 = 7; and 10 – 3 = 7. I would ask questions such as, What do you notice in this pattern? and Why is that happening? These were really hard questions for my children to address, particularly the first graders. However, I felt that they were important questions to ask during our exploration of algebraic thinking, even if the children couldn't answer them.

As we moved forward, I looked for situations that would enable me to ask questions that I thought might help the children make generalizations that fit into my notion of algebraic thinking. In doing this, I floundered around a lot. The discussions were hard, and they didn't seem to affect any of their other mathematical thinking. I began to wonder how all of this was going to serve the children. I wasn't sure what I was expecting, but the questions still felt important to me.

I tried to think about how I wanted students to benefit from this algebraic thinking. I realized that for a first or second grader, what is useful about understanding that you can systematically change an expression (12 + 8; 11 + 9; 10 + 10) is being able to use these ideas to make computation easier. We explored some sets of story problems that I wrote. The problems in each set were related as in this example:

> **?** Andrew was fishing. He caught 17 fish before lunch. Then he caught 5 fish after lunch. How many fish did he catch that day?

> **?** Corey went fishing also. He also caught 17 fish before lunch. He caught 6 fish after lunch. How many fish did Corey catch that day? Is there a way you can use the previous problem to help you with this problem?

Engaging in these types of questions felt helpful to me, and I was pleased with the work we did. But by the end of the year, I was still left wondering where all of this fit into the typical mathematical agenda for my first and second graders.

I am fortunate to teach a multiage class and have all of my students for two years. This situation allows me to revisit questions that do not get answered during a particular year. In many ways, that is exactly what I did this year.

Kate

GRADE 2, FEBRUARY

Throughout this year, I have wondered, What kind of foundation did I lay last year? Did that work benefit the children, and if so, how? And what do I need to do to follow up on that work? I knew that this year, my task with the second graders was to really work on helping them to develop more efficient computation strategies. Would any of last year's work help?

These questions became evident to me in the middle of the school year. We continued to have discussions about ideas that I thought were algebraic, and the children were more efficient in their addition strategies. I wasn't sure about how these two ideas were related, so I decided to have a discussion that might help me to think about this more.

Previously, the children had told me all the things they knew about the number 100. One thing they knew was that you could make 100 in many different ways, and they rattled off this series of equations: 99 + 1 = 100; 98 + 2 = 100; 97 + 3 = 100; 96 + 4 = 100. I decided to start the discussion with this because we had spent so much time last year discussing similar patterns. I thought if I started at a familiar place, it might help me understand the students' skill base.

I started by asking the children what would come next if they were to continue the pattern, and they offered 95 + 5 = 100 and then 94 + 6 = 100. I asked them if they could find the words to explain what was going on in that set of number sentences. Molly started us off.

MOLLY: Well, you are taking a number.

TEACHER: Which number are you taking, the 100?

MOLLY: Yea. And then you are adding zero. And then you take ninety...(she stopped herself here and changed what she was saying before she finished saying 99) 1 number less than the 100 and 1 number more than the zero.

As I heard what Molly was saying, I knew I had to make a decision about how to record her thinking. I could write 100 + 0 and 99 + 1, because that was the context we had been thinking about. However, last year, I felt like sometimes continuing to use the context we had been exploring made the class more confused instead of making the ideas clearer. I wondered if they were ready to move to more of a generalization. Molly was trying to be more general when she stopped herself from saying 99 and instead said, "...1 number less than the 100 and one number more than zero." I decided to try to write what I had heard her say in the most general terms that still reflected her words.

TEACHER: So I am going to call this "any number." (And I wrote those words on the board.) We have any number plus zero (I write "any number + 0") and then you're saying that we take "any number" and we subtract 1 from it (I write "any number − 1") and then you add what to it?

MOLLY: Well, you have a number and then you take away 1 less, like you have the 100 and you take away 1 less and it's 99, and then for the zero, you get that 1.

TEACHER: So instead of the zero, you add 1.

SCOTT: Yeah, you've got to have 1 more than the zero.

Molly and Scott were both talking me through this, and they were carefully watching how I was recording what they said. The chart looked like this:

any number   + 0
any number − 1 +

Now Scott told me that I needed to, "put 0 + and the 1" so that it read:

any number   + 0
any number − 1 + 0 + 1

I was blown away by how quickly Scott and Molly moved to this level of abstraction. Had our earlier discussions helped us to get here? I restated what they had said, and Scott added, "We're taking away from that number and adding to the other number." I wanted to hear if the rest of the class understood what was being said, so I asked for someone to restate this idea. I was met with silence. This was really hard work. Scott repeated that we were subtracting it from one number and adding it to the other. I thought that if the class saw a model of what was happening, it would enable some students to verbalize what I thought that they understood.

I asked Scott to show us what we were doing using a stack of ten cubes to demonstrate instead of 100. He took one off of the stack and moved it onto a second stack and continued to do this, showing one stack getting smaller and the other getting larger.

Kate

GRADE 2, FEBRUARY

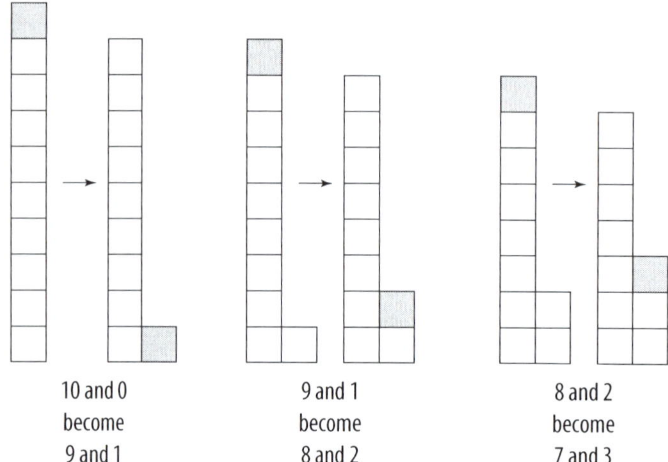

Now, Heather was ready to restate Scott's thinking. She started by saying, "He was saying if you take one off of the 100 and going down to 50 it's always... " and then she trailed off. But now several children were able to finish and restate what Heather was trying to say, and they agreed that you were taking 1 from one pile and adding that 1 to the other pile. Carol clarified that the amount that it equals stays the same, but you keep adding more to the other side.

I was happy with what this discussion was telling me about the students' understanding. They had learned something important about the operation of addition. In fact, when I asked if this would always work, with any numbers, one child said, "Yes, because you're not putting any more on and you're not taking any away." This was reminiscent of the discussion we had had a few days earlier about whether the order in which numbers are added affects the sum. When I asked if it sounded familiar, the children did recall the earlier discussion.

While I was delighted with this level of understanding, my real goal was to help students make their understanding useful. The next question I asked was whether they could use the idea they came up with to make an addition problem easier. Could they change the numbers in a problem so the numbers would be easier to work with, and yet, get the same answer? Students worked to find the sum of 39 + 14 and many were eager to share their ideas.

TREVOR: Put the 10 from the 14 on the 39 and that equals 49.

TEACHER: So you're taking a big chunk. You're going to move 10 over here and make that into a 49. Plus what?

TREVOR: 4. 49 + 4

TEACHER: Now wait. 49 + 4, that doesn't seem easy enough to me. Can you make it even easier? (Several children were bursting to tell me how to do this.) Trevor, can you make it even easier?

TREVOR: You take 1 off the 4 and plus the 3 that's left.

TEACHER: Okay, you take 1 off the 4 and what do you do with it?

TREVOR: Put it over there.

TEACHER: (Pointing to the 49) And what does this turn into?

TREVOR: 50

TEACHER: So, 50 plus?

TREVOR: (Confidently) 3

TEACHER: So, raise your hand if, all of a sudden, 50 + 3 feels a lot easier than 39 + 14. Raise your hand if you know 50 + 3.

Most students knew this fact and were excited to share their knowledge. I posed the question, "What did Trevor do to change 39 + 14 into an easier problem?"

COREY: He took a 10 off the 14 and made the 39 a 49.

TEACHER: So he took 10 away from here (pointing to the 14) and he added it to here (pointing to the 39). Is that kind of like what Molly said, you can take one away from here as long as you add it to that side?

MANY STUDENTS: Yeah.

COREY: Then, he said 49 + 4 = 50.

ANDREW: (Who was listening carefully) 49 + 4 does not equal 50.

COREY: I mean...I forget.

ANDREW: It's plus 1.

CAROL: He took 1 from the 4 and added it to the 49 and got 50. Then he had 3 left on that side and added it to the 50 and it's 53.

Kate

Grade 2, February

Teacher: So here's my question. Is this something you can always do? Start with one problem and change it around this way to make an easier problem? Can you always take some off of one number and add it to the other and still get the same total?

Many Students: Yes!

Molly: Because you're still using the same amount, the same numbers. You're just changing them around.

Teacher: Molly used a really important word the first time she said this. She said, "You're using the same amount." You're using the same amount. I still have these same cubes here, right? And it doesn't matter if I put some here and some here. Do I still have the same amount?

Class: Yeah.

Teacher: Am I taking any away?

Class: No.

Teacher: Am I putting any more on?

Class: No.

Heather talked us through how she changed the problem to 39 + 1 + 10 + 3. Molly shared a strategy that some people thought was complicated and didn't make it easier. Scott shared a solution that broke the 9 from 39 into 6 + 3 and then added 14 + 6 = 20; 20 + 30 = 50; and 50 + 3 = 53. We kept ending up at the same last step, and one child remarked that the last step was easier.

So I am left thinking about what brought us to this point. These children are clearly developing strategies that make their computation more efficient. Were they able to change 39 + 14 into an easier problem because they had generalized that $a + b = (a - x) + (b + x)$, and they felt so certain about this property of addition that they could apply it confidently? Was it because they had developed a habit of generalizing, and could move from the example of addends of 100 to the problem 39 + 14? Was it because I specifically asked them to use their generalization to make the computation easier? There is another way to think about this that keeps running through my mind. Would we have ended up here if any of those pieces had not happened? Was there one part of the process that made the difference, or was it the presence of all of them that mattered?

C A S E 9

Is it two more or two less?

Monica

GRADE 4, NOVEMBER

When I realized my fourth graders were having difficulty with subtraction, I thought about a context that would help them figure their way through problems they encountered. We had been using grams on balance scales to weigh shrunken apple heads and record the weight that was lost over time due to evaporation. During the month that we repeatedly weighed the apple heads, my students had to do a lot of subtraction to find the change in weight. I expected this context would be one they could refer to in future situations to help them think through particular subtraction problems.

During a ten-minute math session on Halloween, I gave them a series of problems to think about. "Pretend these are apple heads," I suggested. "The first number is the starting weight of the apple, and the second number is the next weight. How much weight was lost?" My students had no trouble with the first problem I gave them, 145 – 100. The next problem I gave them was 145 – 98.

For this problem, the students came up with two different answers. The discussion that ensued promised to take much longer than the ten minutes I had allotted, so we returned to the problem later in the day. At that point, many students thought the answer was 43. After all, 145 – 100 = 45 and so, they thought, because 98 is 2 less than 100, 145 – 98 should be 2 less than 45. These students listened intently as others explained why they believed the answer was 47.

Jillian explained that she had realized that the answer was the same as 145 – 100 except for a difference of 2. She tried adding the 2, got 47, and checked her answer by adding 47 + 98 to get 145. At that point, she realized that 47 was the correct answer, and she was satisfied. "You just add it back, and it works," she said, confident that because her answer was correct meant the strategy was also correct.

Lorenzo explained his written process this way, "I did 40 + 98 = 138. I know that because 98 + 10 = 108; 108 + 10 = 118; 118 + 10 = 128; 128 + 10 = 138. Then, 138 + 7 = 145. So, the answer is 40 and 7. It's 47."

Several other children offered their ways of thinking about the problem. Meanwhile, rambunctious Brian was waving his hand in the air, insisting on explaining his thinking, too. He struggled to find the words. "It goes with the problem before," he declared. "It's like you've got this big thing to take away, and then you have a littler thing to take away so you have more. Can I draw a picture?"

I nodded, and he came up to the board, thought for awhile, and then drew a big blob like this:

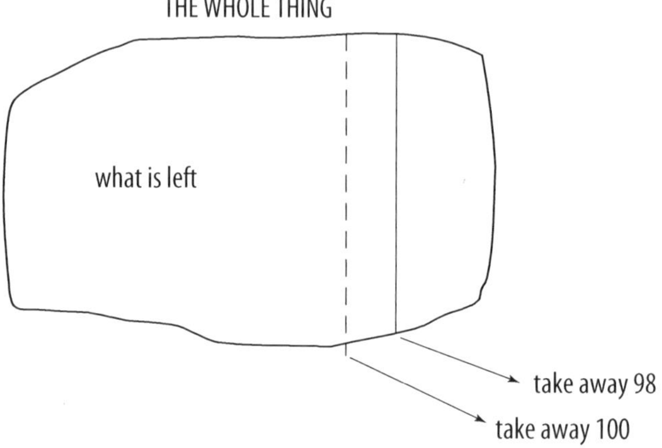

"See, this is the apple at first, " he explained. "And you take some away and have some left. Then you take away 98 grams instead, so it's over here." It appeared to me that Brian had a very clear mental image that was helping him think his way through the problem, but that he was having a hard time verbalizing it to us.

His classmates were watching and listening fairly intently, however, and inspired by his presentation, Rebecca said excitedly, "Yeah, it's like you have this big hunk of bread, and you can take a tiny bite or a bigger bite. If you take away smaller, you end up with bigger."

"Do you think this will always be true?" I asked. "I think so," she answered. She recorded her thinking on her paper in this way:

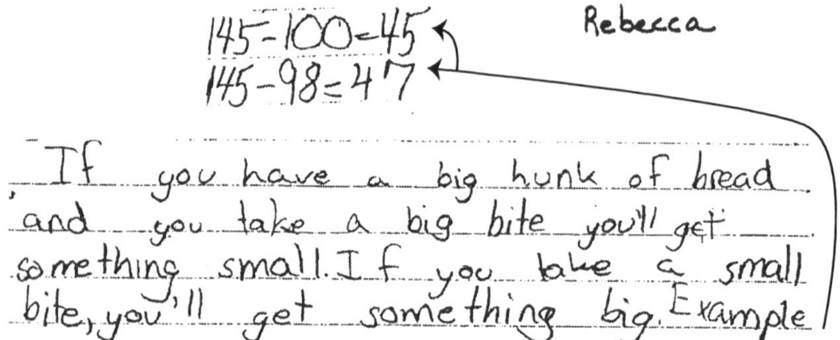

Monica

GRADE 4, NOVEMBER

Up to this point in the discussion, Max had been quiet, although he had correctly figured out early on that the answer was 47. However, he seemed inspired by Rebecca's explanation and Brian's picture. He continued with the thinking that was unfolding when he raised his hand and said, "Yeah, the less you subtract, the more you end up with. AND..." he continued with great emphasis, "in fact the thing you end up with is exactly as much larger as the amount less that you subtracted."

I realized we had devoted another 45 minutes to this discussion, and the lunch bell was about to ring. I asked if anyone else wanted to comment quickly, and Riley raised his hand. Having experienced several moves in the past two years of school, he is a student who is caught between trying to remember procedures he doesn't understand and trying to catch up to his classmates who are more accustomed to reasoning about the operations. He often feels lost during math discussions, but today he seemed eager to get involved. "I used to think it was 43," he said, "but now since I saw it on the calculator and heard everyone talk, it's 47, but I don't get why."

Often Riley was completely lost during these discussions, but this time I suspected he was actually on the brink of understanding. "Let's think about a different context," I suggested. "Pretend it's not apples, but pennies. You have 145 pennies, and the first time I take 100 from you. Now, you have 145 pennies again, but this time I take 98."

A huge smile broke across Riley's face. "Oh, now I see," he said happily, confirming my expectations. He added, "It's like you replay it in your mind, and now it makes sense." Like Brian, he now seemed to have a mental image that helped him solve the problem. When he handed his paper in, I could tell he had corrected his original answer of 43, and that he had darkened the whole problem as if to reinforce his new understanding.

It didn't surprise me that my students had to struggle to understand the relationship between the two subtraction problems. I know that one of the tricky things about subtraction is understanding when to add on the extra amount and when to take it away to arrive at the correct answer. What fascinated me, however, was the depth and variety of my students' thinking about this problem, as well as the intensity with which they thought about it and the widely differing mental images that supported their understanding. I was also interested in the natural tendency children like Rebecca and Max seem to have toward generalizing their understanding in an algebraic way.

CASE 10

$37 + 16 = 40 + x$

Carl

GRADE 7, JANUARY

I am curious to know how my students might use their understanding of estimation to reason about whole numbers in equations and what arguments they can develop to explain why their strategies work. Our curriculum includes some formal work with equation-solving later in the year, and I think that working on their estimation skills will help students with the solving of equations. It might also give me some insights into what they do and do not understand so I can better support them when we get to that point in the curriculum.

I began by explaining, "The ability to estimate often requires a better understanding of mathematical ideas than does the ability to follow a procedure to get an exact answer to a problem. This is why our state standards not only expect that you find exact answers but also that you can estimate and reason with problems. The knowledge and skills you gain through this kind of work will help you to better understand and use algebra which, as you know, is a major focus of our learning this year. So, I am going to give you some equations for which I want you to use estimation and reasoning strategies to solve. See if you can come up with at least two different ways to do the problems."

I wrote on the board, $37 + 16 = 40 + x$, and asked the class to estimate the value of x without calculating $37 + 16$. After a few minutes of individual work time, I gave students about 5 minutes to share their answers and strategies within their small groups.

As I went around the room to listen in on small-group conversations, I noted that some students used strategies they knew produced estimated values, and some students used strategies they knew gave exact values. There were others who thought their estimates were exact answers but were not sure.

To start the whole-group discussion, we listed the values for x students had found: 25, 20, 15, 14, 13, 11. Then I decided to ask a few students with estimated answers to present their work so we could discuss how to know if a strategy results in an exact or an estimated solution. I recorded students' strategies on the board as they shared them.

Michael: Well, you can round 37 to 40 and 16 to 20, so 37 + 16 is about the same as 40 plus 20. So the answer is about 20.

Teacher: Why did you say "about 20"?

Michael: I increased the 37 and the 16 so my answer is going to be bigger; x is less than 20.

Julia: I saw that 37 had been increased to 40 and so I decreased 16 to 15. So I think x is 15.

Teacher: Is 15 an estimate or an exact answer?

Julia: I am not sure.

Michael: Her answer is too large. It is like my problem. She increased the 37 by 3 and decreased the 16 by 1. She added more than she subtracted, so it can't be the exact answer.

Teacher: (To the whole group) What is Michael saying?

Jacob: 37 plus 16 is going to be a number. If you change 37 or 16, you are going to change the number.

Deacon: Julia increased the 37 by 3 and decreased the 16 by 1, so she is still 2 too high.

Teacher: Interesting. I want to come back to this in a moment, but I want to get out a few more strategies first. As you hear the different strategies, I want you to think about whether the strategy results in an estimate or an exact answer and how you know.

Amelia: I rounded 37 to 35 and 16 to 15. 35 plus 15 is easy to add. It is 50. 50 is an estimate. I took away 2 from 37 and 1 from 16 so 50 is three less than the actual answer. 50 plus 3 is 53. But I know that 40 plus x is going to be 53, so it is pretty easy to see that 40 plus 13 is 53.

Jorge: I did something like Amelia. I rounded 37 to 40 and 16 to 20.

Carl

GRADE 7, JANUARY

Jorge came to the board and wrote

37 + 3 = 40
16 + 4 = 20

JORGE: (Pointing to the 3 and the 4) I added 7 to the problem, so now I need to take 7 away from 60 to get 53. And as Amelia said, it is pretty easy to see that 40 plus 13 is 53. So, the exact answer is 13.

KATE: Can I share mine? I got the exact answer, too.

TEACHER: In just a moment. (From my earlier observations of the work groups were doing, I already knew I wanted Kate to share last because I thought that her strategy would provide a good way to get at some of the critical ideas underlying this work. But first, I wanted to make sure students were clear about Jorge's thinking.) I am wondering where Jorge got 7 and 60.

NIKKI: He added a 3 and a 4 to the problem so that is 7 more. The 60 is 40 plus 20.

JORGE: Yeah, so I have to take away 7 from 60 because 60 is too big.

TEACHER: OK, Kate.

KATE: I noticed that 40 is 3 more than 37, so I took 3 away from 16 to get 13. 13 is the answer.

I wrote on the board:

37 + 3 = 40
16 − 3 = 13
37 + 16 = 40 + 13

TEACHER: So why does this work?

KATE: Umm... Ummm... I add 3 so... It is kind of hard to explain.

A number of students began talking at once, indicating that they now thought the exact answer was 13.

TEACHER: I want everyone to look at Kate's strategy. Look up here. (I point to what I have written.) Many of you now agree that 13 is the exact answer. I want you to talk in your small groups about the following two questions: (I write these on the board.)

1. Why does Kate's strategy work?
2. Will Kate's strategy work for any numbers that we might add?

You may want to try some other examples or use diagrams or other representations to help you with this. I am going to give you five or six minutes.

As I went around the room to listen to small-group discussions, I focused on students' arguments. To start the whole-group discussion, I went back to Jacob's previous idea of 37 plus 16 becoming a number.

TEACHER: Jacob, I listened to your group, and you continued with the idea of 37 + 16 being a number. What are you thinking?

JACOB: 37 plus 16 is going to become a number. That number has to be the same as 40 plus x. If you add to 37, you are changing the number, so you have to take away the same amount to change it back.

DEACON: It is like you have piles.

TEACHER: What do you mean by piles?

DEACON: 37 and 16 is a pile of stuff. If you add 3 to 37, you have made the pile bigger. To keep the pile the same, you have to take 3 away from the 16.

JORGE: It is like balancing things out. Whatever you add, you have to take away or the problem is not the same.

As I am writing about this classroom episode now, I realize that Deacon's and Jorge's ideas are something to return to. I'd like to see the "pile of stuff" and have them demonstrate how 37 + 16 can be transformed to an equivalent amount. We can use the "pile of stuff" to illustrate Kate's strategy and consider whether it works for any numbers we might add. But in the moment before I could comment, Tammy raised another issue.

TAMMY: I found an example where it doesn't work. Our group does not think this works with zero, fractions, or decimals. Like 27 + 3. If you add 3 to 27 you get 30, but if you take 3 from 3 you get nothing, so it won't work.

Carl

GRADE 7, JANUARY

The class erupted with talk as many students were saying that in fact this did work. This raised the issue of zero and what zero means. Was Tammy thinking that with zero, the problem did not have two terms?

So in tomorrow's lesson, after we return to the "pile of stuff," we will also take on the claim of Tammy's group. What happens when $27 + 3$ is transformed to $30 + x$? What is the value of x? Does Kate's strategy work for fractions and decimals? I also noted that another group had written $14 + 0 = 17 + x$, which takes us into negative numbers. We will have plenty to discuss as we think about the domain for which our claims apply.

CHAPTER

3

Reordering Terms and Factors

CASE 11	Does order matter when counting?	Lola	Kindergarten, January
CASE 12	Does order matter when adding?	Kate	Grade 2, February
CASE 13	The "switch-around" rule	Alice	Grade 3, September
CASE 14	Switch-arounds for multiplication	Alice	Grade 3, January

Early in their work with numbers, many students notice that when two numbers are added in either order, you get the same sum. Students often make up a name for this generalization; for example, they might refer to it as "switch-arounds." To us, their generalization sounds like the Commutative Property of Addition.

However, when students are asked whether this will always work, it seems that often they have something different from the Commutative Property in mind. On one hand, some students are unsure about whether it is a claim one can make for all numbers. After all, it is impossible to check every number. On the other hand, some students think about switch-arounds as a rule to be considered for all operations. If switch-arounds work for addition, do they also work for subtraction, multiplication, and division? Once students figure out for which operations switch-arounds work, they often extend their rule to apply to any order or grouping of multiple addends or factors.

In Case 11, a class of kindergarteners discusses whether it makes a difference if you first count the black checkers or the red checkers when you want to know the number of checkers in a jar. In Case 12, second graders work to *prove* that order does not matter when adding a pair of numbers. In Case 13, a teacher of third graders comes to see that a term like *switch-arounds* can mean different things to different students. Later in the year, in Case 14, the same third-grade class considers how to model the switch-around rule for multiplication.

As you read the cases, consider your own images of these properties. How do you understand the way the Commutative and Associative Properties operate? How might you illustrate them?

CASE 11

Does order matter when counting?

Lola

KINDERGARTEN, JANUARY

In the Counting Jar this week there were eight checkers—three red and five black. The children "visited" the Counting Jar at various times during the week and counted the checkers. As usual, they recorded their counts on index cards using pictures, numbers, words, or a combination of these. Then they created another set of objects with the same number of items as there were checkers in the Counting Jar.

I did not spend a lot of time at the Counting Jar this week. We had several other math activities that were new, and the children are used to the routine of the Counting Jar. I looked over their index cards and spot-checked a few of their collections. Everyone seemed to have gotten eight for their count. Only two students, Jannah and someone who neglected to write his/her name, indicated anything about the checkers' colors on their cards. Jannah showed three reds and five blacks, and the other person showed four reds and four blacks.

Lola

KINDERGARTEN, JANUARY

At the end of one math period, we met on the rug to discuss the Counting Jar. Alejandro counted the checkers for us. At first he started to count them any old way, and then he stopped and sorted them by color. He counted the reds first and then the blacks: 1, 2, 3...4, 5, 6, 7, 8. We reiterated that there were eight checkers and determined that there were three red checkers and five black checkers.

Then I posed a big question and told the class I wanted them to really think about it for a minute. "If someone else were to count the checkers and count the blacks first and then the reds, would the total be the same?"

There was, as there fairly often is, a feeling of many students having an immediate response, either verbal or nonverbal. Many of the immediate responses seemed to be affirmative, but I definitely heard at least one or two students say no. As usual, when I scanned the class, there were students who looked a bit unsure, too.

Marisa was one student whose nonverbal response made it clear that she was sure there would still be eight checkers. I asked her about it and she said, "I think you will [still end up with eight], but instead of counting the three first, you'd count the five first."

Tom also thought you would get eight but said he didn't know why. Danielle said if you put the red first and then the black or the black first and then the red, they'd be the same. I asked why, and she said, "If you took one away it would change it, but if you didn't, it would be the same." Several children then demonstrated taking one checker, or one of each color, away and counted to show that the number of checkers changed. Although nobody commented about adding a checker to change the total, I think some children were having the thought that if you don't actually change the total by taking some away or adding some in, you will have the same amount regardless of what color is counted first.

Emma said that she counted the blacks first and got nine. I asked if she remembered Alejandro's count when he counted the reds first, and she did. I asked if she thought that if you count them in the other order, it could be a different number, and she said she wasn't sure. She was the only one to actually express this uncertainty, although it is likely that other students were also unsure.

Jake said it would be eight whether you counted the reds first or the blacks first. I asked why, and he counted the set both ways, red first and then black first, and got eight both times. "See?" His demonstration applied to this very set of objects.

Lola

KINDERGARTEN, JANUARY

I posed a new question to the class: Is getting the same total no matter which order you counted something special about the checkers, or would it work with anything? Students who murmured or nodded immediate responses thought it would work with anything. I'm not sure if any of the silent, still students were thinking something different.

Amber said, "If you take the same number, it would be the same." Amber demonstrated her idea with yellow and blue teddy bear counters. I helped her put out 3 yellow teddies and 5 blue teddies. Amber counted the 3 yellows first and then the 5 blues and got 8. I asked Craig, "What if you count the blues first?" and he said, "Eight," without hesitation. I asked how he knew that, and he said his mother taught him. Ariel demonstrated another way to count that still yielded eight: yellow, blue, yellow, blue, yellow, blue, blue, blue.

I asked if this was something special about the number eight, or if it would work with other numbers. No students commented on this. We did try counting a set of 3 blue and 3 green color tiles. The class as a whole seemed bored when we got 6 no matter which order we counted. This conversation was getting way too long for many of the kindergartners, but I really pushed on WHY? WHY? WHY? Marisa said, "It doesn't matter how you do the colors, it matters how many there are."

So, it seems that some students have some understanding of "order not mattering" when counting a set of things that can be thought of as two subsets. It is difficult for them to articulate why, and many of their statements apply to the example at hand. And, as always, I am unsure about students who aren't saying anything, as well as students who nod along once they get a feeling for the group consensus.

I decided to speak to some students one-on-one, specifically the seven students who didn't say anything in the whole-group discussion. Tony counted the whole set each time. Blues first, count them all by ones; reds first, count them all by ones. Lisette, however, laughed when I switched the order of her two color groups. She is a quiet girl whose first language is not English. But she laughed and said, "No change!"

CASE 12

Does order matter when adding?

Kate

GRADE 2, FEBRUARY

I was about to have a discussion about whether it matters in what order two numbers are added. I was interested to see what would be said in this discussion because when this question was raised earlier in the unit, the children seemed sure that the answer was no but didn't say much to back up their thinking.

Since that time, we have talked about breaking numbers apart into chunks and putting them back together in different ways. We also discussed whether counting a set of objects by numbers other than one affects the total. We have had several more weeks to talk about the work they are doing on Today's Number. It seems to me that there has been a shift in the children's thinking throughout this unit. Most of them are operating on a numerical level, and there are far fewer children who need to count on in order to do computation. I wondered if these experiences would affect this discussion. Does operating numerically reflect the potential to think more abstractly about these ideas? And, what is the expectation for a second grader answering this question anyway?

On the day prior to this session, I introduced a question to the class. I asked the children to think about an activity that we had done involving coupons. "If you wanted to save 30, what are two coupons you could have? Let's think about coupons that come in chunks of fives and tens." Someone offered 20 and 10. I then asked if we wanted to combine 20 and 10, would it matter if we added 20 + 10 or if we added 10 + 20? I was answered with a resounding no. I wish I could describe the certainty and engagement in their voices as they all started to tell me why. I told them that the next day we would spend some time showing how they knew that this was true.

The following day, I restated the task and explained my expectation for what it means to "prove" what you are thinking. I told the children that to prove it meant to convince someone. For example, if the principal came in and they had to convince him that what they said about the order was true. I told them they could use any tools they needed to help explain their ideas. I listed cubes, diagrams, and number lines as possible options, and I sent them off in pairs to work on their proofs.

Last year, when we worked on proving ideas like this, I was continually surprised that the children could speak with certainty about something being true but not be able to explain why. This year, they had already demonstrated the certainty. Would they get beyond that? Would it feel more satisfying this time?

We came back together as a group after about 15–20 minutes of partner work. Some children brought cubes or base-10 blocks to help explain their thinking, and some brought written work. I wanted to make sure that they could get past the notion that "because we all know this, there is nothing to explain." So, I began the conversation with this reminder. "When you are doing your explaining, I want you to pretend that Mr. Valen is standing here and that he doesn't believe you, so you've got to be really careful to convince him. Don't assume anything. Say all the things you need to prove it." I chose Kathleen to start us off because she is someone who often fits into the category of saying something is true but not being able to say why. This time, she had found a way to express why and brought a clear diagram with her.

KATHLEEN: If you take a 10 and a 20 and then you switched them around, it will just equal the same thing. You put the 10 in one place and then you put the 20, and you put the 20 where the 10 was.

TEACHER: Can you show people your paper, Kathleen? You showed your thinking with a picture, right? So, hold the picture up and show us what you mean by "if you put the 10 where the 20 was." (It felt to me like pushing for this kind of connection between the representation and what she was saying was key to their level of proof. I really wanted to push for specificity.) Can everyone see Kathleen's paper? So what do you mean, if you put the 10 where the 20 was?

Kate

GRADE 2, FEBRUARY

Kathleen held up her paper and pointed as she talked. "Like right here, the 10 goes here and the 20 goes where the 10 was." She was pointing to her diagram of 10 cubes in one section and 20 cubes in the other and then showed switching them, as if she were moving the cubes.

TEACHER: And why is it that it doesn't matter, Kathleen?

KATHLEEN: Because it's like any way you switch it, it would just be the same thing. Like, any number you could probably do it with. You could probably do it with any number. (As I listen to this again on tape I am struck by the word Kathleen chose to use, *switch*. Implied in *switch* seems to be a change in position but no change to the quantity or value. I am also struck by the fact that the children are so used to thinking about "will it always work" that I didn't have to ask that question this time.)

Kate

Grade 2, February

Teacher: So, are you saying that you think it would work with any number? Like with any two numbers you could switch them, and it won't change the answer?

Andrew: Any, any number.

Teacher: Andrew, you are agreeing that with any, any number you can do that?

Kirsten: Like 17 and 33.

Sally: And you don't just have to use two numbers.

Teacher: (I decided to focus on the any number part of the discussion before we moved on to more than two numbers.) Like any two numbers, like 17 and 33.

All of a sudden three or four students were talking at once, telling us that it could be any numbers and that it could be more than two numbers. Andrew even said that you could use a billion numbers. I tried to get all of the ideas heard.

Teacher: So, Kirsten said you're just switching to a different spot. Molly, what did you say?

Molly: I said you didn't have to use only two numbers.

Teacher: You didn't have to use only two numbers.

Kirsten: I know you could use 10 and 5 and 3.

Teacher: Wow, you could use three numbers like 10 and 5 and 3?

Molly: You could use eight numbers.

Kirsten: It doesn't matter.

At this point, there were students joining in and talking all at once saying that you could use more than two numbers, and in fact, it didn't matter how many numbers you used. Even a billion numbers! Something about this feels like a whole other level of generalization to me. Not only does it work for any pair of numbers, but students also have such a clear idea that the order doesn't matter, they know it will not matter regardless of how many numbers are involved. So why are they so sure? We had seen very few representations to back up their ideas, and I wanted to get back to that. I knew that Corey, Marissa, and Paul had thought about this in a more generalized way so I called on them to continue the discussion.

They had brought base-10 blocks representing the number 140: one 100-flat and four 10-rods. Corey explained that they were adding 40 and 100.

COREY: You're just switching them around (switching the position of the blocks on the carpet) and not putting any more on or taking any away. You're not adding some, or you're not taking any away. You're just switching them around and putting them in different spots.

TEACHER: OK.

MARISSA: And you also can break the numbers up only if you don't take any or add any more on.

TEACHER: Marissa, can you say more about that? You can break the numbers up as long as you don't...

SCOTT: Yeah.

MARISSA: ...take any away or add any more on.

So now we seemed to have moved on to a bigger concept. You can move the numbers around or break them up, and as long as you don't add any additional cubes on or take any away, the total number of blocks will stay the same.

TEACHER: So as long as you don't take any away or add any, you can also break the numbers up?

COREY: (Pushing the blocks into a different configuration) Yeah, this could be 10 + 10 + 100 + 10 + 10.

TEACHER: You could call that (pointing to each block as I said it) 10 + 10 + 100 + 10 + 10. Would you guys agree with this? What do other people think? Do you agree?

I was answered with a lot of yeses.

COREY: It could also be 10 + 10 + 10 + 10 + 100.

TEACHER: And then he could say 10 + 10 + 10 + 10 + 100, and you wouldn't have to add it again, you would just know it is 140.

STUDENTS: Yeah.

COREY: Because four 10s and 100 is 140.

Now I continued the discussion of more than two addends but shifted the context.

TEACHER: I hear a lot of people saying that not only do you feel really certain that this works with two numbers, but there are a bunch of people who feel really certain that this works with more than two numbers.

VOICES: Yeah.

TEACHER: Let's say we have three numbers. Let's say we have 6 + 4 + 2.

I wrote the numbers on a board.

TEACHER: Someone said that was 12. So you are telling me that automatically you'd know 4 + 2 + 6? You'd know that answer without trying it?

SCOTT: 12.

TEACHER: You're sure about that?

VOICES: Yeah.

SCOTT: Because add the 6 and the 4 up and then the 2 up (showing the work on paper that he did with Heather). Well, the first one has a 6, a 4, and a 2, and the second one has a 4, 2, and a 6.

HEATHER: It's exactly the same.

SCOTT: Yeah, you switch around the places of the numbers.

Several students joined in by sharing number sentences with these three numbers in different orders. Scott continued by showing us that it was true because each way he entered the numbers into the calculator, it still came out 12.

TEACHER: Scott, you are showing us that the calculator says it's true. I'm wondering if anyone has a way to absolutely prove it not just because the calculator says it's true but because it absolutely has to be true. (It is so hard to find the words to explain what it means to prove it. No wonder it's hard to figure out if they did.) Not because I say it's true, but you can prove it and convince Mr. Valen.

HEATHER: (Talking at the same time as others) Because you're not putting any more on or taking any away.

TEACHER: I heard Heather say something that was like what Corey said. Can you say it again Heather?

HEATHER: You're not putting any more on, and you're not taking any away.

I reminded them that this sounded like what Corey and Marissa had been talking about earlier. Maura shared that she tried several examples and it worked each time. Kirsten and Carol shared what was written on each of their papers.

Kirsten

10+20=30

20+10=30

It dasint matr becose It is just Swiching. It is int oding or tacing away It is the Same

Kate

GRADE 2, FEBRUARY

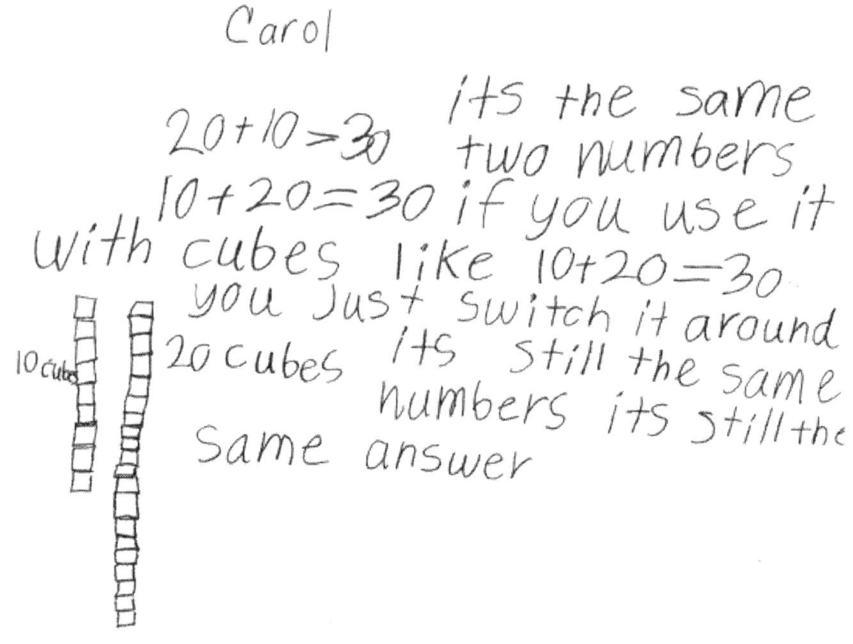

When we started this discussion, I wondered if it would be different than conversations that we had had in the past. I think it did have a different quality to it. Something about this discussion made me feel satisfied that these children had generalized the property and proven it. Partly, it was that they articulated the piece I wanted to hear—nothing additional was added and nothing was taken away. That feels like a big piece of the mathematics. The other part was that they connected the idea that order doesn't matter to the related idea that you can break the numbers apart and move the parts around without affecting the total. If children find the generalization to be true in other circumstances, they truly accept and understand the "theory" of the generalization.

C A S E 13

The "switch-around" rule

Alice

GRADE 3, SEPTEMBER

DAYS ONE AND TWO

My class began exploring the Commutative Property of Addition when we looked at the 10s facts. Some students represented the facts as 0 + 10, 1 + 9, 2 + 8, 3 + 7, 4 + 6, and 5 + 5, and then they said, "You can just switch them around for the other ones." Based on that work, the following day I asked them if 0 + 10 was the same as 10 + 0. As a group, they decided the answer was yes *and* no: "Yes, because they are the same numbers and they equal the same, 10; but no, because they're in a different order. They're not in the same spots." I wanted to push them on this a bit more. So, with their input, I recorded our "switch-around" rule and asked them how sure they were that the rule would always work, even with numbers other than the 10s facts. The rule, I wrote was:

> When you add two numbers together, you can change the order and still get the same total.

Four students were not sure if it would always work, six students were pretty sure it would always work, and nine students were positive it would. Two students were absent.

When I asked them how they were thinking about this, they started to give examples of number facts in which they knew the rule worked: 10 + 2 = 12 and 2 + 10 = 12; 9 + 7 = 16 and 7 + 9 = 16; 10 + 20 = 30 and 20 + 10 = 30; 19 + 10 = 29 and 10 + 19 = 29; 2 + 7 = 9 and 7 + 2 = 9; 5 + 2 = 7 and 2 + 5 = 7; 4 + 3 = 7 and 3 + 4 = 7. Everything seemed to confirm that our rule worked in all the situations we tested.

Ben said, "I have one that doesn't work: 3 – 2 = 1, but 2 – 3 = 0. " Allan disputed the 0 answer and said it was ⁻1, but Ben's point remained the same, and others agreed. They believed our rule did not work. Karen offered another example, "5 – 3 = 2, but 3 – 5 = 2." Ben said, "A minus won't work unless it's the same number." I was astonished that no one was bothered by this discussion because our rule clearly stated, "When you add...." Susan did claim that we weren't talking about subtraction. Although most disregarded her comment, I underlined the word *add* when she said it.

What had happened? The rule I had written stated, "When you add two numbers together..." but many students were thinking about both addition *and* subtraction. That afternoon, as I reflected on the discussion, I realized that I had written the rule in my words, even though I believed at the time that I had merely restated their words. The next day, I asked them to write the "switch-around" rule in their own words and give examples to show if it's always true, sometimes true, or rarely true.

Their comments helped me to see that the term *switch-around* meant different things to different students.

- If you switch around the numbers in a math problem, you will get the same answer. I think it's true, but I'm not sure about division.
- The switch-around rule says 2 − 1 = 1 and 1 − 2 = 1.
- It's always true, like 10 + 1 = 11 and 1 + 10 = 11. The same. And 100 + 20 = 120 and 20 + 100 = 120. Wherever the numbers are, they're the same.
- The switch-around rule is you put two numbers together and you switch the numbers and it equals the same thing, like 7 + 3 = 10 and 3 + 7 = 10, 100 + 700 = 800 and 700 + 100 = 800, 30 + 40 = 70 and 40 + 30 = 70, 3 + 27 = 30 and 27 + 3 = 30, 6 + 5 = 11 and 5 + 6 = 11, 1000 + 8000 = 9000 and 8000 + 1000 = 9000.
- The switch-around rule is an example that 3 + 7 = 10 is the same as 7 + 3 = 10 and 5 − 3 = 2 but 3 − 5 = ?, so it does not work for some number sentences.
- The switch-around rule is when you take two numbers and add them together and try switching them around. Say you had 5 + 3 = 8. You would switch them around to 3 + 5 = 8. For 5 − 3 = 2, then switch them around to 3 − 5 = $^{-}2$.
- The switch-around rule says that if you take, let's say, 6 + 4 = 10, then that means 4 + 6 = 10 and yes, it is always true.
- The switch-around rule is if you have two numbers and you put the numbers in the other one's place, it will equal the same thing, but you

Alice

GRADE 3, SEPTEMBER

can't use subtraction, otherwise it will not work, like 4 + 5 = 9 and 5 + 4 = 9, but 8 – 7 = 1 and 7 – 8 = $^{-}1$.

- 10 + 20 = 30 / 20 + 10 = 30. The switch-around rule isn't true because 3 – 2 = 1, but 2 – 3 is naguiv 1, so it isn't true, so there! 4 – 5 = naguiv 1.
- The switch-around rule is when you change the order of the two numbers that you add and still get the same total. Example:
  1. 6 + 4 = 10; 4 + 6 = 10
  2. 5 + 5 = 10; 5 + 5 = 10
- The switch-around rule is if I have say 3 apples and 4 plums, if instead I said I have 4 plums and 3 apples it will still equal 7 pieces of fruit.
- It's true but not true because 5 + 6 = 11 and 6 + 5 = 11, but 5 – 6 = $^{-}1$ and 6 – 5 = 1.
- When you add or subtract 2 numbers and you switch them around, you get the same total. Most of the time true 8 + 7 = 15 and 7 + 8 = 15, 8 – 7 = 1 but 7 – 8 = 0. I think the switch-around rule works only when you add.
- It's like if you added 5 and 7, you get the same answer either way and it's always true except for minuses like 7 – 3 = 4. Switch it around and it's 3 – 7 = 0.
- The switch-around rule says that you can switch around the numbers in addition 5 + 6 = 11 and 6 + 5 = 11.
- I think it's always true. The switch-around rule is when you take two numbers and add them together. Here's an example: 3 + 6 = 9 / 6 + 3 = 9. The only way the s.a. rule won't work is if you use multiplication or subtraction or division; but if you take two of any of the same numbers of those sections of math, then you get the same answer.
- The switch-around rule says that no matter which way they're put, they equal the same.
- The switch-around rule says you can change the order of the numbers. It works every time you add two or more different numbers. [Like to add] 5 + 7 + 3 [first you can add] 7 + 3 = 10 [and then] 5 + 10 = 15 [or if you wanted to add] 4 + 8 + 1 [you can add] 8 + 1 = 9 [and then] 9 + 4 = 13. [To add] 8 + 9 + 4 [first add] 8 + 4 = 12 and 12 + 9 = 21. [To add] 7 + 3 + 4 + 1 [first add] 4 + 1 = 5 and 7 + 3 = 10 [and then add those] 5 + 10 = 15.

Alice

GRADE 3, SEPTEMBER

DAY THREE

After examining what students wrote, I knew I wanted to have a conversation that would help the class come to an agreement on what this rule would mean and to which numbers and/or operations it would apply. I began the next class discussion by asking the students to tell me what the switch-around rule meant.

TEACHER: Yesterday, people had such interesting ways of talking about the switch-around rule in their writing. Is there anyone who would be courageous enough to offer one to start us off? Is there anybody who thinks she or he has one that we could listen to, so we could take it in and revise it until we have something that we think we all could agree with? (Hands go up. I call on Karen.)

KAREN: (I write as she speaks.) The switch-around rule is two numbers put together that if you switch them around, they still equal the same thing.

TEACHER: Comments?

KAREN: Oh, for example, $7 + 3 = 10$ and $3 + 7 = 10$.

TEACHER: OK. Comments? Sharon, what do you want to do with this?

SHARON: I think that it should be that...um that the switch-around rule...um...only works...I think that it only works when it's plus.

TEACHER: Karen, is that any place in your definition already? That it only works with addition? Is that something we have to add to what you've already said?

KAREN: Umm. (Long pause)

TEACHER: Can someone say what it is that we're trying to think about here? What is the issue that Sharon has brought up?

CHRIS: What Sharon is saying? I think she's saying that it can only work with pluses, but it can't work with minuses because it can work like with $7 + 3$, but $7 - 3$ would, but $3 - 7$ wouldn't work. No, wait, it would work with both because...you could do neg...nega.... Cause there are some numbers below zero. Well, you use numbers below zero.

Here, I think Chris has gotten tangled up in the confusion about the possibility of negative numbers and what we are meaning by the word *works* in the situation of the switch-around rule. Some are saying that 3 – 7 won't work, meaning you can't do it, and others are saying that 3 – 7 is either $^{-}4$ or 0, and so it doesn't work because it isn't 4. I'm a bit unsure how to proceed with that confusion. At some point, they need to know that 3 – 7 is not zero, that it is $^{-}4$. Most are not yet ready for this work, so even though it seems like an interesting and important idea, I decide to bring the group back to Karen's words.

TEACHER: Can I ask something? How many people would agree that if we're talking about addition, the switch-around rule works all the time? (I read the rule as Karen said it.) Raise your hand if you're sure that it's always going to work for addition.

MARK: Do you mean for every number in the entire world?

TEACHER: For every number in the entire world.

CHRIS: Two different numbers?

TEACHER: Two different numbers, two same numbers... Add them together, switch them around, they're still going to equal the same amount.

Many hands go up.

TEACHER: Raise your hand if you're not sure.

STEVE: If you're not positive?

TEACHER: Yup.

Two hands go up. One is Steve's and the other is Marina's.

TEACHER: So, Marina, what do you think would convince you? What are you still not sure of that would make a difference to you?

MARINA: Well, I'm not too sure it will work for *every single* number because...

STEVE: Because we haven't tried every single number.

KAREN: I don't think we should use negatives because it's not really about them. Our rule is just like...about...like positives.

Alice

GRADE 3, SEPTEMBER

TEACHER: Are you convinced that our rule works for addition when we're using numbers zero and above? We still haven't tried every number.

MARINA: I'm more convinced.

STEVE: Yeah, me too, but I'm not sure.

SUSAN: I haven't tried every number, but I'm convinced because I know that if it works with some of the numbers, it will probably work for other ones because you're still using the same numbers. It's like if you did a handstand, your body would still be the same; it's just upside-down.

FRAN: Oh, yeah, like if I did a handstand, I wouldn't turn into Susan!

Giggles come from the group. They seem to like this image. I do, too, and so we end the discussion on this note.

I am wondering how much progress we have made. Because this is our first experience developing a rule like this, I have to believe it is time well spent. Some important ideas did come up, and I think they will help us as we develop other rules for the operations.

One of these ideas is that we can establish the realm of numbers for which our rule will hold true. Even though I think there was some confusing conversation about negative numbers, eventually Karen suggested that we exclude negative numbers from our consideration. I tried explicitly to let them know that we could do that because we were developing the rule to fit what we knew about numbers. I wonder how arbitrary this process seemed to my students. How narrowly could we limit the range of numbers and still have the rule be useful?

Another component was the idea about how many examples are needed before you can say a rule will work every time. What does it take for the generalization to be validated for all numbers, even ones that have not been tried? Does the absence of an exception allow such a claim? In my class, Marina and Steve were uncertain. I wanted to acknowledge their skepticism and have the rest of the class notice that they had accepted the rule even though they had not tried every number. I liked that this issue was put on the table.

One last suggestion was the possibility that we could return to our rule and revise it. I liked thinking that as we examine more operations and other numbers (negative and rational, for example), we can return to our rules and see if they still hold true or if we can revise them so they still apply to other kinds of numbers.

Although I am sure this discussion did not completely establish these ideas as components for all the work we will do for this year, I do believe it will provide us with a foundation for future debate and discussion as we develop other rules for how the operations work. I was surprised by how quickly such an apparently "simple" property as commutativity (which students actually use all the time without thinking about it) became so difficult to articulate and so difficult to understand as an abstraction. Also, I was taken aback by how challenging it was for some students to think about a property of *addition* rather than a statement about what you can do with numbers regardless of the operation.

Still, we have a first draft of our rule posted in the classroom, and just the other day, as we began our work with multiplication, somebody said, "Three groups of four or four groups of three. They both equal twelve. It just switches around!" That may just be the opening I was looking for...

CASE 14

Switch-arounds for multiplication

Alice

GRADE 3, JANUARY

My students had come up with the term *switch-around* in the fall to describe the relationship between 5 + 4 and 4 + 5. Although I mentioned the term *Commutative Property* (I do want them to hear the language of mathematics), they preferred to use their own term. We continued to talk about the switch-around rule.

Although in September there were questions about all of the operations, at that time they were looking primarily at addition. Now that we were working with multiplication, I thought they would be interested in reconsidering this idea. I asked them to find a way to convince someone that the switch-around rule works for multiplication. The class worked in pairs and used a variety of models for representing multiplication. After watching them work, I thought about the sequence of presentations for the sharing session. I wanted to have the discussion build in such a way that it would be coherent and sensible. In my mind, I had categorized the models they had used into three kinds: arrays, skip-counting, and grouping.

Three partner groups had developed models based on arrays to show how turning the picture or snap-cube configuration would not change the total.

Martha and Mark had drawn rectangles. One was 3 by 20 and the other was 20 by 3. I asked them to share first.

MARTHA: This shows three groups of 20 and this way it shows twenty groups of 3.

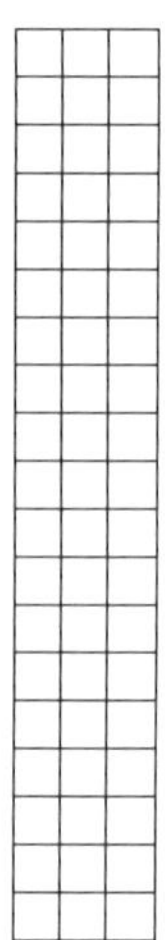

three 20s

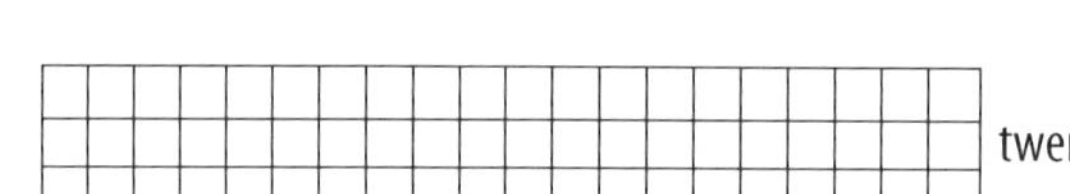

twenty 3s

TEACHER: What makes you think this will work for any numbers, not just three groups of 20 and its switch-around?

MARK: Because we tried more, too.

TEACHER: Did you try all the numbers?

MARTHA: No, we didn't have time, but we're really convinced because we really just know because if you have 4 × 6, you'd have the same as 6 × 4, but also it could be a hundred or a thousand or anything. It would have to work.

SUSAN: I think that's because it's not one of those patterns you have to see all of it to know. I think it's one of those patterns that if you see that it works on most of them, it will work on all of them, and then you just know it's going to work for every single one.

Teacher: Does anyone else have a model that's similar to this one? Marina, how about you and Holly and Mary?

Marina, Holly, and Mary used a layered representation. They built one array as ten sticks of 3 and the other as three sticks of 10, and then put them on top of each other to show how they matched up exactly.

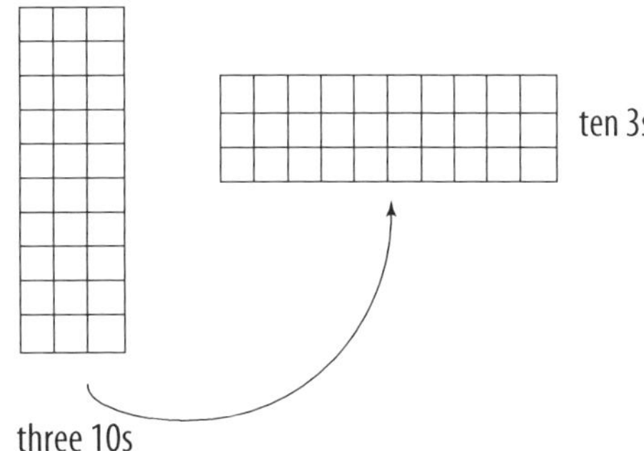

Marina: (Showing their snap-cube construction) This is 3 times 10. We made this layer of ten 3s, and then the layer of three 10s and it fits right on top.

Daniel: The bottom layer is ten 3s and the top layer is three 10s, and they fit.

Marina: It means it works.

Teacher: How do you know that it works for numbers other than 3×10?

Susan: (Again, restating her claim) I think this is just one of those patterns you know works all the time, not like one of our "Theories under Construction" where we might find ones that don't work. But I'm not sure if it works for fractions and negative numbers.

Teacher: Todd and Allan, your model seemed similar to Marina's. Can you show us that next?

Todd: This is a 5 by 4 array, and if you turn it, which is what the arrow shows, you get a 4 by 5. This one is 5×4, and it equals 20, and this one is 4×5, and it also equals 20. The 5 from here (pointing to one side of the array) goes here (pointing to the other dimension) and the 4 from here goes to where the 5 was. It's still 20.

ALLAN: We used the arrow to show turning. We thought of switching as turning.

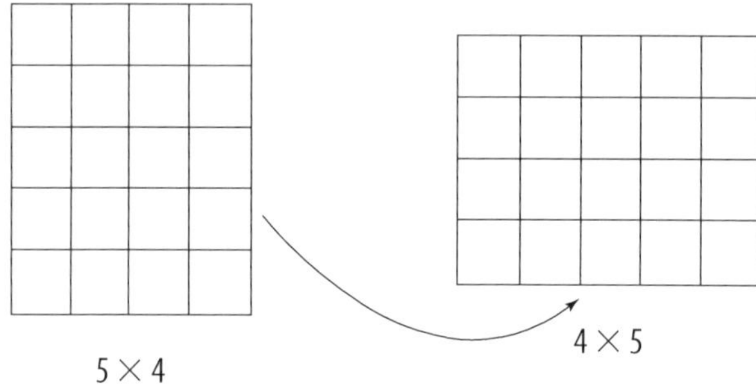

I was trying to figure out, as they talked, if they noted that their methods would work no matter what the numbers were. However, each time I asked, the students told me about their thinking with specific numbers. I am still wondering about this. I turned to another group.

TEACHER: Fran and Daniel, what would you call your model?

FRAN: The skip-counting model. We can show how it works if somebody gives us a multiplication problem.

STUDENT: 3 × 12

FRAN and DANIEL: So we do three counts of 12: 12, 24, 36. Then, we do twelve counts of 3: 3, 6, 9, 12, 15, 18, 21, 24, 27, 30, 33, and 36. And we get the same answer.

DANIEL: So that's how we can use skip-counting. We just do it with the numbers that are in the multiplication sentence. We just do it that number of times.

TEACHER: So are you saying that one number becomes the number you're counting by, and the other number is how many counts and then you switch it?

DANIEL: Then the second number becomes the number you count by and the other number becomes the number of counts. It has to always work.

Alice

GRADE 3, JANUARY

The last method for showing the switch-around rule for multiplication was grouping. Sharon and Karen devised this method. They first put the snap-cubes into sticks of six. Each stick was a different color. They made ten of these to show 10 × 6, or ten groups of 6. Then they dealt out 1 cube from each stick into each of 6 groups. The transformation showed how 10 "six-sticks," each of the same color, became 6 groups of 10, with each of these groups having 1 cube of each color.

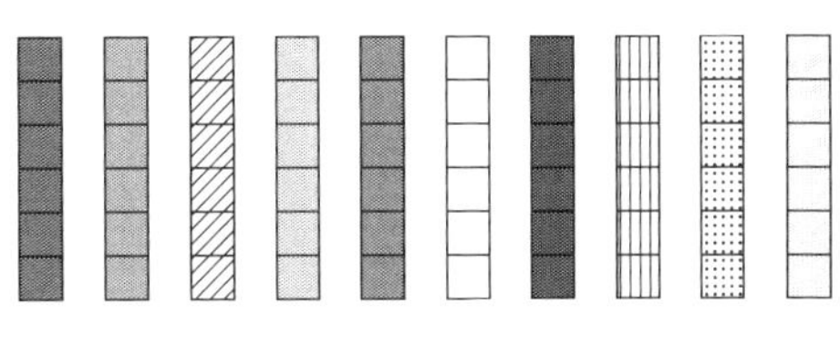

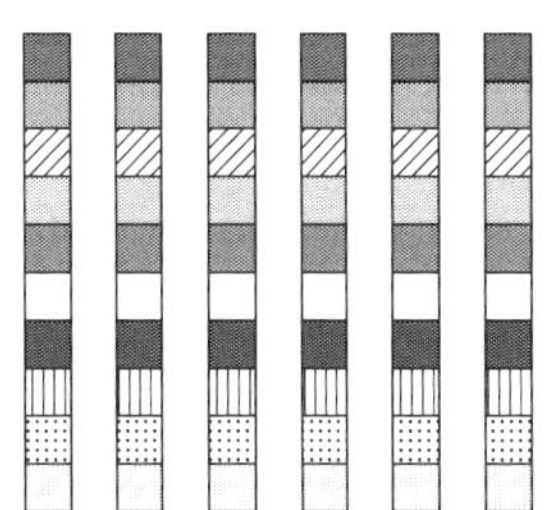

I think their model had great power because it demonstrated what appeared to be a dramatic transformation as the switch happened, going from many sticks of the same color to fewer multicolor groups. It really surprised the class that in spite of the very different look of the "before and after" configurations, nothing of the quantity had been lost or gained. Their surprise indicated to me that this idea of switch-arounds, which they all said they believed, is still being worked on.

As I reflected on this sharing session, I began to understand how I could better structure and plan for the learning experiences I want to provide for my students. Asking students to focus on convincing someone, rather than just finding number examples, made the level of engagement different and much more inclusive. Everyone, even those who had not yet arrived at a workable model, brought enough of a context to the discussion so as to be able to connect with the ideas being presented. By comparing each other's models to their own, they were able to think about how they were similar and different.

Also, there was a different air of confidence in the arguments my students posed this time. By creating models, they had convinced themselves of something that they were ready to "go public" with. We still need to work on just how "general" this generalization is. Do their models include the possibility that the numbers might be fractions or very large or even zero? How can we bring up the almost hidden assumptions they might be making about what kinds of numbers we are working with? We will continue to work on these ideas, but this was a good beginning. Through both the creation and presentation of their models and representations, students came to understand more about this property of multiplication and what it means to make a convincing argument.

A question I am still left with is whether the three models are equally convincing. I find the array model offers the most convincing demonstration that multiplication is commutative. No matter what two whole numbers I start with, if the multiplication is represented as an array, I can view it as n rows of m squares ($n \times m$) or m columns of n squares ($m \times n$). Do the other representations allow me to picture why $n \times m$ and $m \times n$ will always result in the same product?

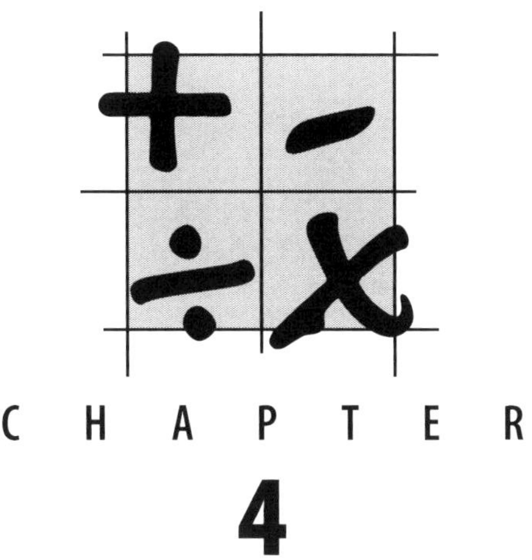

CHAPTER

4

Expanding the Number System

CASE 15	Is zero really a number?	Alexandra	Grade 1, December
CASE 16	12 cats and 0 dogs	Cassie	Grade 1, November
CASE 17	Multiplying by 0	Michael	Grade 5, May
CASE 18	It has basements	Katrina	Grades 1 and 2, April
CASE 19	Does the order rule still hold?	Lucy	Grade 3, March

A third-grade teacher describes the start of a mathematics lesson in April.

> The class had previously talked about whether or not whole numbers could be added in any order, and I wanted to know if they trusted what they had learned about addition and whole numbers to also work for fractions. I put the following expressions on the board:
>
> $\frac{1}{4}+\frac{1}{2}$ $\qquad$ $\frac{1}{2}+\frac{1}{4}$
>
> I asked the students, "If you add these, will you get the same amount?"

This teacher is aware that the generalizations her students have made have all been in the context of whole numbers. However, as they now bring into view new kinds of numbers—in this case, fractions—they must reconsider their generalizations. Do they still hold? Often, as with the case of commutativity, they will find that the generalization does hold in an expanded number system. However, at times, they will have to refine their generalizations to account for the new class of numbers. For example, many students believe that multiplication "makes things bigger" except for the special cases of 0 and 1. However, when they begin work on multiplying fractions, they find more exceptions. They learn that $\frac{1}{2} \times \frac{1}{4} = \frac{1}{8}$; that is, the result of the multiplication is less than both factors. Now, in the context of fractions, they will need to further refine their generalization about the behavior of multiplication.

In this chapter, students are confronted with numbers that are new to them, and they work to make sense of an operation applied to these numbers. In Case 15, students, who have up to now encountered the idea of number through counting—1, 2, 3, 4,... —are now considering whether zero is a number. In Case 16, first graders work to extend their argument for switching the order of addends to include zero. Though these ideas may be settled in the primary grades, we see in Case 17 a class of fifth graders working to extend their notions of multiplication to include zero.

In Case 18, a group of first and second graders take initial steps to think through what numbers less than zero might be. And in Case 19, third graders reconsider the idea of reordering addends when using these new types of numbers. When negative numbers are included, can you change the order of addends and still get the same sum?

As you read the cases, you may find that you also need to revisit assumptions and generalizations you have made about numbers. You will find it helpful to take note of these ideas.

CASE 15

Is zero really a number?

Alexandra

GRADE 1, DECEMBER

The students were discussing how they wanted to set up the "Birthday Board" to indicate the birthdays of students in the class. They decided that each month would have a marker with the birthdays of their classmates listed.

Alexandra

GRADE 1, DECEMBER

It was noted that some months have no student birthdays. January was one of these months, so they agreed that January would have zero markers. All seemed well until a student commented that January had no markers, and so there was nothing there, so 0 is not really a number. I seized the opportunity.

I gathered the class on the rug for a whole-group discussion.

TEACHER: Do you think 0 is really a number?

CARRIE: It is really a number, but it equals nothing.

JACK: It is because you put it on the school day count chart.

MICHAEL: It is a number, but it doesn't equal up to anything.

BETTY: No, because no one's birthday is on a 0.

ED: If you counted by 0s a hundred times you'd have nothing. $0 + 0 = 0$.

RACHEL: It equals zero.

TEACHER: Does it matter as a number?

CLASS: No, not really.

TEACHER: Does the last day of school matter?

CLASS: YES!

TEACHER: At the end of the year, we have 3 days of school left and then 2 days left, and then 1 day left. Would we ever have 0 days of school left?

CLASS: It counts then.

TEACHER: Why doesn't it count the rest of the time?

CLASS: Ohh, that's tricky. (They really did say this in unison.)

TEACHER: Does it matter if I say 0 ice creams after lunch?

CLASS: Yes, it matters!

TEACHER: You can each have 0 birthday parties this year!

CLASS: NOOOOO!

TEACHER: It matters when it comes to birthdays?

CLASS: Yes.

Alexandra

GRADE 1, DECEMBER

I am not sure what we figured out today. This discussion opened up questions for me. What does it mean to students when they say a number "counts" or "matters"? As a group, the class said zero matters when it means the lack of something, such as no birthdays or ice cream. What is it that students need to understand to accept that zero is a number?

CASE 16

12 cats and 0 dogs

Cassie

GRADE 1, NOVEMBER

My first graders have been exploring ways to decompose numbers into two parts. Early in the year, they were asked to find how many peas and how many carrots make 7 vegetables all together. Later, they were asked how many blocks and how many marbles make 9 toys all together. Last week, we were working on different ways to solve a similar problem involving 12 pets, counting only dogs and cats. The students worked with a partner using different manipulatives, including their fingers, to solve the problem in a variety of ways. When it came time to share, I told them to pick one solution to show the rest of the class. As they were trying to figure out which one to choose, I overheard Thomas and J.T. having an argument.

THOMAS: This one looks funny, why don't we share this one instead?

Thomas was pointing to a tower of 12 brown cubes and referring to the tower as "funny." He wanted to share the tower that had 7 brown and 5 orange cubes instead. I talked to them and asked them what the argument was about.

THOMAS: J.T. wants to share this one, but it looks funny, so I told him to use this one (pointing to the 7 brown and 5 orange cubes).

TEACHER: Why would you suggest sharing that one instead?

THOMAS: Because it looks right.

TEACHER: What do you mean by right?

THOMAS: It has a little of everything.

I suggested that they share the tower with 7 brown cubes and 5 orange cubes, but I told them to hold onto the tower of 12 brown cubes. I was thinking that would be a good setup for a conversation about the number zero and its role. This was the perfect opportunity to examine students' thinking about this concept.

At sharing time, many great ideas came up. One team presented 4 + 8, and when another team presented 8 + 4, some students noted that was the same combination. "If you are holding both towers together, all you have to do is to 'flip' one tower around, and it would be the exact same thing." Just then, they seemed not to be thinking about cats and dogs, but about the relationship between two numerical expressions: The sum is the same, no matter how you order the addends. I was pleased to hear them noticing and exploring these great ideas.

After everyone had shared a solution, I thought it was time to present the dilemma Thomas was facing earlier.

TEACHER: As you were deciding which combination you wanted to share with the rest of the class, Thomas and J.T. were having a very interesting discussion. They were holding this tower of 12 cubes. J.T. wanted to share it with you, but Thomas thought it looked funny. What do you think of it? Could this be a combination of 12?

NAJLA: I don't know; it has 12, but it has nothing else.

TEACHER: What do you mean by "nothing else"?

NAJLA: It doesn't have any other color.

TEACHER: Was that your thinking, Thomas?

THOMAS: Yes, it only has brown.

J.T.: But it's OK because it has 12.

TEACHER: What was the total we were looking for?

FATIMA: 12, like J.T. said.

Cassie

GRADE 1, NOVEMBER

TEACHER: Does this represent 12?

NAJLA: Yes, but where are the dogs?

Najla was thinking if the 12 brown cubes were the cats, where were the dogs? So, I returned the question to the group.

TEACHER: So, you have all agreed that the brown cubes represent the cats, and here we only have 12 brown cubes. Where are the dogs?

JASON: There is none.

TEACHER: If you wanted to write *none* in numbers, what number would it be?

ASIA: Zero. Zero is none, nothing.

TEACHER: So, you mean if 0 is nothing, and we have 12 cats... Mmm, how many dogs do we have?

REGGIE: We have 0 dogs. Should we say 0 dog or 0 dogs because there is not more than one?

Leave it to Reggie to make a connection to other things we are learning.

ASIA: I think it should be 0 dog.

I wanted to skip the language arts lesson and draw them back to the mathematics of the moment because with this group, one thing can lead to another and before we know it, our day is done. We have to stay focused on the topic.

TEACHER: Let's go back to the combination we are trying to make here. Thomas, with the discussion we have been having, would you agree that could be a way to make 12?

THOMAS: So we would have 12 cats and 0 dogs?

TEACHER: Right, and J.T., how were you thinking about writing the number sentence to match your idea?

J.T.: 12 + 0 = 12

CARMEN: I know, or we could say 12 cats + 0 dogs = 12.

TEACHER: Could we write it another way?

BRIAN: You mean flip it around like the tower?

TEACHER: Yes.

BRIAN: You could write it, but you can't show it.

TEACHER: What do you mean?

BRIAN: Well, if there is nothing, how are you going to flip it?

REGGIE: You can pretend it's on this side instead of being on this side.

Reggie came up and showed us how we could "pretend" to move the 0 from one end of the tower to the other end to make 0 + 12 as well as 12 + 0. It was a hard concept to imagine something there when there was nothing.

TEACHER: So it could be 12 cats and 0 dogs? Do you agree with that, Thomas?

THOMAS: Yeah, it doesn't look funny anymore.

REGGIE: I know, it's like in the book, *Julius, The Baby of The World.*

I knew exactly what he was referring to. We are currently doing an author study about Kevin Henkes. After reading several books of Kevin Henkes's, this one has been the class favorite.

TEACHER: What do you mean, Reggie?

REGGIE: Just like in the book when Lilly said that if her brother was a number, he would be 0 because 0 is nothing.

ASIA: Oh, yeah!

I just thanked Reggie and smiled. He is always making connections. He surely made a point that everyone could refer to.

CASE 17

Multiplying by 0

Michael

GRADE 5, MAY

We have not been working extensively with zero, so I decided to learn more about my students' concepts about zero and its uniqueness. As part of teaching math concepts, I feel that it is extremely important to introduce my students to these ideas about zero. I realize that zero has very special characteristics, and getting fifth graders to recognize this simple notion may be an accomplishment in and of itself.

For this lesson, I decided to deal with zero in the context of multiplication and addition. I placed two examples on the board for students to examine. $6 \times 0 = 0$ and $6 + 0 = 6$. I then asked students to complete a task regarding these problems.

? Record a rule or generalization about multiplying with 0 and another about adding with 0. Do your generalizations always work? Explain why or why not using pictures or diagrams, whenever possible.

As students struggled with this—and they did struggle—I observed many of them working with arrays. However, in setting up the arrays, they were unable to represent zero. Indeed, I am wondering if using zero precludes the use of an array. How does one incorporate the use of an array to help the children with this idea?

One of the most important ideas came from a student as I overheard him suggest to another student that they come up with a word problem that might work. I felt like this was such an integral part of working with zero, understanding it in context, that I introduced this idea to the other students. While it was difficult to interject a new idea midlesson, many of them attempted to find some solutions using a context.

? I have 7 books in my desk. When I went to the store, I didn't buy any books. How many books do I have?

? I have 1 computer. I have 0 hours to play with it. How many hours will I have played in a month?

Michael

GRADE 5, MAY

> **?** Jim has 20 boxes of candy to sell in 30 days. On the first day, he sold 0 boxes of candy. If he continues like this, how many boxes will he have sold on the thirtieth day?

Students generally struggled with understanding zero in a word problem. The notion of constructing a problem around adding or multiplying zero seemed superfluous in that the kids already knew how zero would affect their answer. In spite of this, some students did generate problems that made sense. Zero took on relevance and meaning in the context of these word problems. Tomorrow I'll have these three students share their problems with the class as a way of continuing our work.

CASE 18

It has basements

Katrina

GRADES 1 AND 2, APRIL

In recent years, I have become interested in the number line as a tool to use for computation. I have also wondered about the role that a number line might play in a first and second-grade classroom. Unlike problem solving or computational strategies, I did not think that children would invent such a tool. I think one of my roles as a teacher is to introduce a tool when it might be helpful. I also know that I walk a fine line between, on the one hand, introducing a tool and helping the children to see ways in which it might be useful and, on the other hand, having that tool overwhelm other strategies, such as using cubes, 100 chart, or diagrams, that might make more sense to them in their problem solving.

With all of this in mind, I introduced number lines to my first and second graders. We worked for about a week on what the children noticed about a number line and what it would look like to solve fairly easy problems using this tool. I chose examples like 5 + 3, problems for which they already knew the answers. As they worked with the number line, the issue of where to start counting and where to stop counting came up and gave us the opportunity to discuss those concepts. These are actually pretty big ideas for these children.

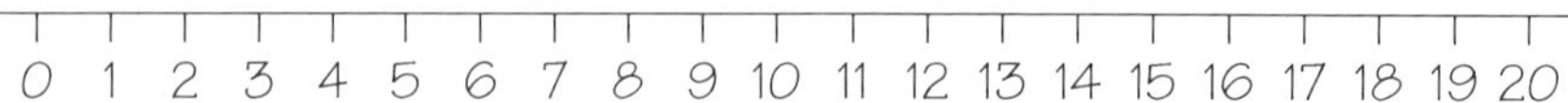

I had decided to work with a number line that went from 0 to 20, but I drew the line slightly extended both before the 0 and beyond the 20. Next, we played a number line game in which players move their pieces up or down a number line by playing one or more of five cards in their hand. The cards have values 1, 2, 3, 4, $^{-}1$, $^{-}2$, $^{-}3$, or $^{-}4$. The object of the game is to capture chips that have been placed on the number line by landing on these chips. We started the first game by placing the chips on the even numbers.

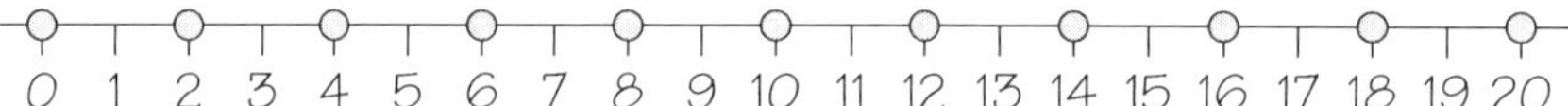

I had some questions in mind before I set the class up to play the game. What would the children make of the negative change cards? I suspected they would see the "–" symbol as a minus sign and not a negative sign since we had not broached the topic of negative numbers yet. I also knew that those tricky negative numbers were just lurking in the background, waiting to spring out at us. Even though we were using a number line that ended at zero, we might well be forced to consider what would happen when we were at zero and got a negative change card. I wondered what sense the first graders, particularly the ones with less developed number sense, would make of these negative numbers. Could they imagine numbers to the left of zero? It might give us something interesting to talk about, or if it was too far out of reach, it would help me think about what kinds of experiences they might need to have that discussion later.

I explained the rules to the class—each person gets five cards and, to start, you place your piece anywhere along the number line. At each turn, you can use as many cards as you want to move your piece, and if there's a chip where you land at the end, you take that chip. Then, you replace the cards you used. We played our first short practice game, teacher versus the class. Most of the children understood which way to move the piece when using positive or negative change cards and where to start and stop counting. They seemed very involved and almost every student was participating.

At first, the chips were plentiful and easy to acquire. The game progressed with each side taking a chip on each turn, until the chips became more sparse. As it became harder to get chips, the children began to think about using more than one card on each turn in order to capture a chip. This was a challenge for some of the children. It was on one of these turns that we had our first introduction to the idea of negative numbers.

The class piece was on 2, and Carl suggested they play two cards, a $^{-}3$ card and a 1 card in order to capture the chip that was on the zero. We were still playing on a number line on which the numbering stopped at 0, but the line continued a bit past that to the left. I was wondering what the children thought about moving $^{-}3$ when they were on 2.

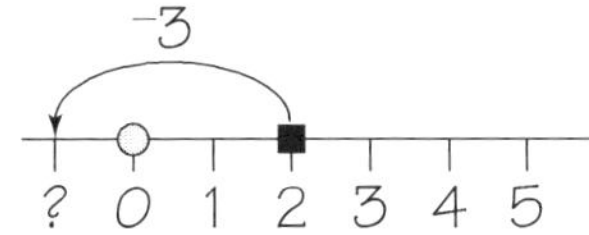

Teacher: Carl was on 2, and he went minus 3?

Carl: So I was on minus 1.

Teacher: He went minus 3. How did he go minus 3?

Carol: He went 1. (She indicated 1 jump to the left.)

Teacher: He went 1, and where did that leave him, Carol?

Carol: 2, he has to move 2 more.

Teacher: One and he had 2 more to go and he went...

Seth: Minus 1.

Teacher: What do you mean minus 1? Where's that? I don't see that on this number line.

Seth: It's 1 below 0.

Teacher: It's 1 below 0?

Heather: It's 0 and you go 1 below.

Teacher: It's 1 below 0. Wow.

SETH: Then he went plus 1.

TEACHER: Then he went plus 1 and it took him right back to 0?

The class was much more quiet at this point, so I let the ideas hang out there for a moment and then asked, "What does anybody think about that spot that Carl and Seth just called '1 below 0'?"

HEATHER: That's minus.

TEACHER: What do you mean that's minus, Heather?

HEATHER: Then minus 1, minus 2, minus 3...

TEACHER: So, you're saying that you think the number line keeps going with minuses?

She nodded.

TEACHER: Irene?

IRENE: My mom and my dad told me that before 0 there's negatives.

TEACHER: There's negatives? What does that mean, there's negatives?

Someone offered, "Like negative 1," but the discussion was dying out. Some children had heard about this phenomenon and a few children seemed to be able to think about $^{-}1$. "One below 0" sounded like what it was, just one space or one jump below the 0, even though it was next to the 0, not actually below it! I was aware that there seemed to be some children who were not participating in this discussion. I wondered if they had any understanding about the ideas being discussed.

I decided it was time to get back to the game and get everyone involved. We began to play again, and I have to say that the fates were with me. I could not have planned for a better setup to return to these ideas. There were only two chips left on the number line, one on the 8 and one on the 10. The class playing piece was on 3, and they had only negative change cards. My piece was on 18, and I had mostly positive change cards. As soon as I saw this, I knew what was going to happen. As the children looked at their cards, they also seemed to have a sense that their moves were now limited in some way.

One of the amazing things about playing this game was how the children began to anticipate the possible moves. When they saw where my piece was and saw my positive cards, the children realized that I could not move to land on any chips. Carol asked, "What are you going to do?" I used two 1s and told the class I did that so that I could be dealt two new cards. It did not help because I drew two positive cards. The students asked if they could have some of my cards, but because they would not let me have any of theirs, I did not agree. This request, however, shows that they had a sense they needed my positive cards, and I needed their negative ones.

It was Heather's turn to play for the class. She wanted to use a $^{-}4$ and a $^{-}3$. I asked where their piece would be if she did that. The students did not answer, but they did strongly object to her suggestion.

TEACHER: You're on 3. What's going to happen if Heather uses these cards?

MOLLY: We're going to be all the way out... I don't know.

At this point, I drew a new number line on the easel and numbered it from right to left, 4, 3, 2, 1, 0. I continued making tick marks past zero but did not number them. I pointed out where their playing piece was (at 3) and asked what would happen if they moved $^{-}3$. We moved back 3 and landed on 0.

ELLA: If we're on the 0 (she points to the 0 on the number line we are playing on) and we minus 4 (she moves her finger over to the left the equivalent of 4 spaces), then you'd be over here (and points to an empty space).

TEACHER: They said if we went minus 4 we'd be on that spot.

CAROL: What is that spot?

IRENE: Nowhere.

TEACHER: Irene says nowhere. Carl, you had a name for that spot.

CARL: Minus 4.

TEACHER: Carl says this is called minus 4. Carl, can you explain to the class why you think that is called a minus 4?

CARL: Because...well, well...I think it's called minus 4 because it's below 0, and in number sentences, you minus 4 so, it's like going down under 0.

TEACHER: It's like going down under 0?

Katrina

GRADES 1 AND 2, APRIL

CAROL: You are going into 0's basement.

TEACHER: You're going into 0's basement? Is that what you said Carol? (I was intrigued by her image of this because I was pretty sure that it came to her on the spot.) Like this is an apartment building and here's 0 and this is its basement?

CAROL: Yeah, it's below 0. And it has basements that go lower and lower.

TEACHER: You think it has basements that go lower and lower?

Some students talked about each number having a basement, that every number has one less than itself, and Carol made a remark that let me know she was still thinking about extending the number line, "It could go all the way to 100 basements."

I was fascinated by what some of the children seemed to understand during this discussion. I was also struck, once again, by how the children's ability to make sense of this was directly related to the development of their number sense. The developmentally younger first graders who still needed to count all, that is, those who were not yet counting on, found it hard to participate in the discussion. The children whose number concept was more developed, who were able to begin to think about something that you cannot really hold or see, could think about places on the number line that were less than 0. I understand why a child who needs five cubes to think about 5 can't think about less than 0 yet.

CASE 19

Does the order rule still hold?

Lucy

GRADE 3, MARCH

As the year has gone on, I have seen my students' ideas about combining numbers grow. In September, they had no question that 6 + 4 and 4 + 6 both equaled 10. They would say the answers were the same because the numbers were just turned around. However, when given a string of 1-digit numbers to add, most would start at the beginning and work their way through in order rather than looking for combinations of 10 or easy sums they knew. So, even though they said they could add two numbers in any order, they didn't extend that idea in their work to make problems with multiple addends easier. I knew I would be paying attention to these ideas as they came up in class in the hopes of creating opportunities for us to think about them explicitly.

Later in September when dealing with a string of small two-digit numbers, almost all would add them in the order written. For example, when adding a string like 25 + 18 + 15 + 22, most students would take apart the 10s and 1s and combine the 20 and the 10 to get 30, then add on the 5 from the 25 and the 8 from the 18 to have a subtotal of 43. They would continue by adding 10 from the 15 to have 53 and then the 5 for a subtotal of 58. Finally, they would add 58 plus 20 for 78 and then the 2 to get 80. I was looking to see if they would notice that rearranging the numbers to something like 25 + 15 + 18 + 22 would make their work easier. A few did this, but it was not common.

In October when the class was faced with figuring out the total after a series of positive and negative changes (What is the result of moving 4, $^{-}3$, 2, 3, and 2?), almost every student would add the digits in order. They would not look for $^{+}3$ and $^{-}3$ in the string to combine them even though they "knew" $^{-}3 + 3$ would give them 0. When asked how they figured out the total change, it was clear that order did matter to them. Many even said the answer would be different if the numbers were in a different order.

In early March, we played Double Compare, a card game in which each player lays down the top two cards from his or her pile and finds the sum of the numbers shown. The player with the highest total wins. In this version, the deck of cards included both positive and negative numbers, and the class was discussing what happens when you add 3 and $^{-}7$. Dina showed on the number line why the answer was $^{-}4$. She started at 3, then moved her finger to the left on the number line as she counted back 7. Harry said it was the same as 3 – 7, the answer was $^{-}4$.

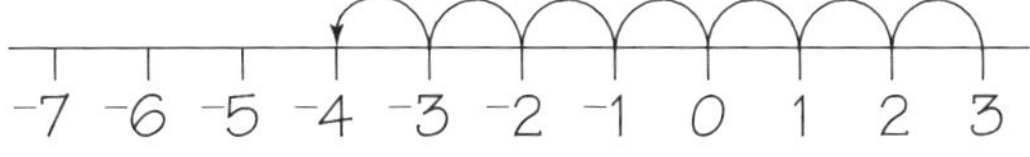

I switched the cards around and asked what the total would be for $^{-}7 + 3$? Jack said it would be the same because we had not changed the numbers. I asked if someone could show us what Jack meant. Amanda showed it again using the number line, this time starting at $^{-}7$, then moving to the right 3, landing on $^{-}4$.

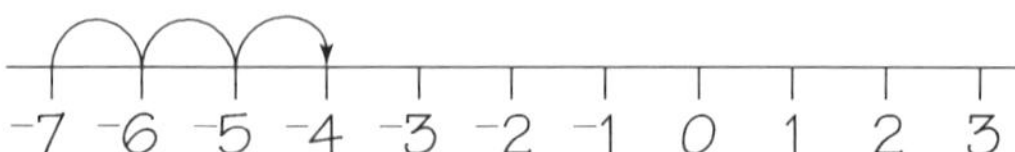

I asked Jack if that was what he meant.

Jack: It is just like the other times when we added. If you don't change the numbers, you won't change where you end up.

Elizabeth: You can think of it as like different distances. Like you can go 3 and then go $^{-}7$ which means you turn around to go in the opposite direction. You'll still end up there if you went $^{-}7$ and then turned around to go 3. You still end up at the same place.

Burt: I could start at 3 or at $^{-}7$ and I would still end up at $^{-}4$ when I use the other number.

It was easy for Elizabeth to make this connection to distances because of the work we had done with number lines. As I write this, I realize how far the class has come since thinking about positive and negative change in the fall when order mattered so much. Would they be so sure if there were many numbers involved? Their ideas about combining numbers have really grown as the year has progressed. In addition, their ideas have broadened to include different types of numbers as well as different situations. Where will they be in June?

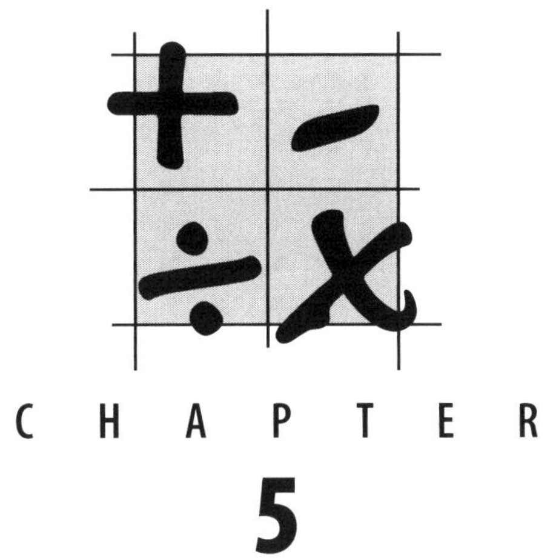

CHAPTER 5

Doing and Undoing, Staying the Same

CASE 20	One situation, two equations, part 1	Azar	Grade 6, September
CASE 21	One situation, two equations, part 2	Nadine	Grade 1, December
CASE 22	Finding a missing change	Daisy	Grade 1, December
CASE 23	Is one acting just like zero? part 1	Alice	Grade 3, December
CASE 24	Is one acting just like zero? part 2	Alice	Grade 3, December
CASE 25	Thinking about negative numbers	Carl	Grade 7, April

A second-grade teacher asked her students to name some expressions that equal 4. One student's expression, 4 + 30 – 30 + 20 – 20 + 2 – 2 + 1 – 1, touched off a discussion about why that works. Among her classmates' explanations were Dan's: "30 – 30 = 0; 20 – 20 = 0; 2 – 2 = 0; 1 – 1 = 0. So, the 4 just stays the same"; and Heather's: "You start at 4. You bounce up 30 and bounce back 30. You bounce up 20 and bounce back 20, and so on. So you always come back to 4."

Students in this class are working with two basic and related principles. First, that subtraction "undoes" addition; that is, they are "inversely related operations." And second, that adding 0 does not change the quantity; 0 is the "additive identity."

In this chapter, we will study cases in which students work on these ideas. In Case 20, sixth graders discuss how the same situation can be represented by two different equations, one involving addition, and the other subtraction. In Cases 21 and 22, we see that the opportunity to begin thinking about these ideas arises even in first grade. In Cases 23 and 24, third-grade students examine the parallel structure of addition and multiplication by discussing the roles of 0 and 1.

In Case 25, we see middle school students taking on some questions from Session 4 by extending the domain to include numbers less than 0 and figuring out how to operate with them. In this chapter, we will examine how the idea of related operations helps in thinking about operations under this extended domain.

As you read the cases, consider how your view of the number system incorporates the ideas highlighted by students' comments.

CASE 20

One situation, two equations, part 1

Azar

GRADE 6, SEPTEMBER

I gave the following problem to my class:

? My scale weighs everything 2 pounds heavier than its actual weight. I packed a box with winter clothes to send to my daughter at college. I weighed the package so that I could find out how much I would have to pay to ship the package. It weighed 8 pounds on my scale. What is its true weight?

Weigh some of your items and record what each will weigh on my scale.

What if a box weighs z pounds? How much will it weigh on my scale?

After my students worked on this problem, I asked that they work with their groups to try to write a rule that would help them find the weight of any object, either its actual weight or its weight on my scale, if one of the weights was known. We agreed that A would stand for the actual weight in pounds, and S, the reading on my scale. This sounded complicated to the students, so the task needed to be paraphrased a number of times before they went to work. After taking some time for exploration, the students came together again and shared their findings.

JOHN: If you know the actual weight, you can add 2 to find the other weight.

TEACHER: How can we express that as an equation or a number sentence?

LISE: We got that, too, but we wrote $A + 2 = S$.

CREE: We got that, too, and we checked it with our chart. See, if A is 6, then $6 + 2$ is 8, and that's S.

All the other groups seemed to agree with Lise except for Patrice's. These students seemed to be puzzled.

TEACHER: But I noticed that Patrice's group has a different rule.

PATRICE: Yeah, we got $S - 2 = A$. But, it's wrong.

TEACHER: What does your rule say?

PATRICE: It says that you take the weight on Ms. Scott's scale and take away 2 and then you have the actual weight. But, it must be wrong.

TEACHER: What don't you like about it?

JOSEPH: (Who was in Patrice's group) But wait... That's not wrong, only different. Sometimes you have to add, and sometimes you have to subtract.

TEACHER: But, how do you know when to do each?

PATRICE: I don't know.

Joseph realized that the two equations are equivalent and both describe the situation of the scale. Patrice seemed to think that only one equation could be correct; and because John, Lise, and Cree's explanation seemed convincing, her own equation must be incorrect. In order to make the issues more explicit for the class, I feigned confusion (a stance I sometimes take, which they are used to).

Azar

GRADE 6, SEPTEMBER

TEACHER: I'm confused, too. I know that addition and subtraction are different. How can these be the same? I'm really confused now.

JOSEPH: It depends on what you want to know. Do we want to find the actual weight or the weight on your scale?

TEACHER: What difference does it make?

JOSEPH: (Undaunted by my questioning) If you know the weight on our scale, you use our rule. Then you can find the actual weight. If you know the actual weight, you can use Lise's rule because then you can add 2 to get the other.

TEACHER: Can someone explain what Joseph has said? I think I'm still a little confused.

PATRICE: Me, too!

The discussion continued in this manner until most students seemed to understand the equations and were able to explain what the letters represented and how the rules worked.

Patrice still seemed confused, however, and I reminded myself that not everyone has the same level of understanding at the same time. I noted that I would check back with her group the next time we worked on writing rules for problems.

CASE 21

One situation, two equations, part 2

Nadine

GRADE 1, DECEMBER

I began the lesson by showing my students five counters and an upside-down paper cup. Students were told that some of the counters would be hidden underneath the cup. They needed to look at how many counters were still outside the cup and then try to figure out how many were hidden under the cup. This was an easy task for my students because the number 5 was such a small number. Then I sent them off in pairs to play the same game with 9 counters.

As the children worked, I circulated around the room recording the strategies that they were using. I found the work of a particular pair very interesting. Carmen knew immediately how many counters were under the cup, but her partner, Inez, was having difficulty. Before I could step in to help, Carmen found a solution to the problem. She put 8 counters under the cup, leaving 1 counter outside the cup. She helped Inez count on from 1 to 9, using her fingers, to determine that there were 8 counters under the cup. Next, she put 7 counters under the cup with 2 outside and again helped Inez. She continued with this sequence until Inez was feeling successful. At this point, I moved on to record the strategies of the other groups.

The next day, I was eager to discuss the strategies my students used to figure out how many counters were under the cup. To begin the discussion, I showed the class another example. There were 9 counters all together, and 3 were outside the cup. How many were under the cup? It was not long until all of their hands were up. Everyone agreed the answer was 6, so I asked for the strategies they used to find the answer, and I recorded them on chart paper.

Sheenah: I started out with 10 fingers. I put 1 down to make 9. Then I put down 3 fingers and I got 6. So, I recorded it.

I made sure that Inez shared her strategy.

Inez: I put 3 in my head and counted up using my fingers until I got to 9. I counted 6 fingers.

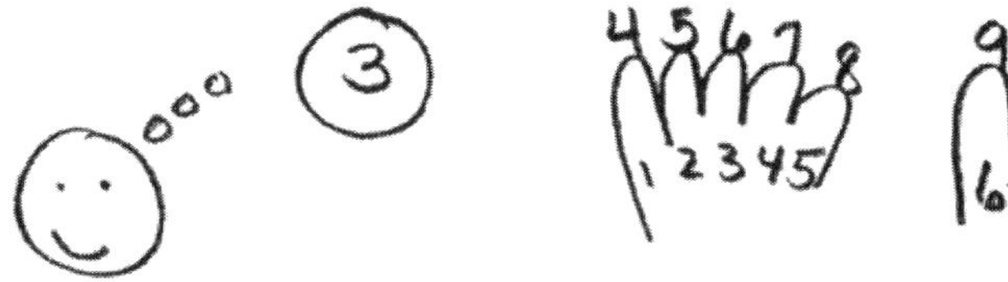

I took this opportunity to point out to the class that Sheenah started with 9 and Inez started with 3, but they both got the correct answer. Why?

Kevin: What difference does it make? The numbers are the same and they stay in the same order whether you go down or up.

Kevin went to the board and wrote:

9, 8, 7, 6, 5, 4, 3, 2, 1, 0
0, 1, 2, 3, 4, 5, 6, 7, 8, 9

His explanation was simple but seemed to be an eye-opener for many. I went back and asked if anyone could come up with a number sentence for both Sheenah's and Inez's strategies. The equation for Sheenah's strategy was $9 - 3 = 6$ and the equation for Inez's strategy was $3 + 6 = 9$.

I heard this comment from Kevin: "Hey, they are the same numbers but in different order."

Kevin asked to come to the chart to show what he meant. This is what he wrote:

$9 - 3 = 6$
$3 + 6 = 9$

With this information on the chart, a few students started noticing things about the equations.

"I noticed that the highest number is the first one in the subtraction problem."
"I noticed that the highest number is the last one in the adding problem."
"I noticed that 9 doesn't make sense if it's in the middle."
"I noticed that 3 and 6 can be anywhere but not the 9."

This last idea was explained further when Maria showed us:

$3 + 6 = 9$	$9 - 6 = 3$
$6 + 3 = 9$	$9 - 3 = 6$

I recorded all of the above information on the chart, but we were running out of time. We will continue with these ideas another time.

C A S E 22

Finding a missing change

Grade 1, December

My class has been very receptive to exploring mathematical concepts this year. Recently, I decided to explore missing addends to see if that leads us into thinking about how addition and subtraction are related.

I presented the problem:

? There were 5 students in the classroom. Some more students walked in. Now, there are 7. How many students walked in?

I asked the students to think about the problem for a few minutes before we began the discussion.

Teacher: So, how many students walked in?

Andrew: 8

Teacher: Why?

Andrew: 5 and 7 is 8.

Teacher: Can you show us how 5 and 7 is 8?

Andrew held up his fingers showing 5 on one hand and 3 on the other (6, 7, 8). I was very confused about what Andrew was thinking. He was very matter of fact with his answer. Could he have been counting up 1 more past 7 to get to 8?

Teacher: I am confused how you got your answer.

Andrew: See, if you have 5 here, then 3, there's 8. So the answer is 8.

I decided to move on to see if another child's response would help Andrew. I am still not sure what Andrew was actually doing.

Ellie: 12. 12 kids came in. There's 5, then 7, so that is 12.

Teacher: Ellie, I want you to read the problem to us again.

Daisy

GRADE 1, DECEMBER

Ellie is a good reader, so I felt comfortable asking her to read the problem on the chart to the class.

ELLIE: There were 5 students in the classroom. Some more students walked in. Now, there are 7. How many students walked in? See, Mrs. Price, first there is 5, then 7. So there's 12.

I saw that Ellie was looking at the two numbers and immediately combining them. I do not think that Ellie was thinking about what was going on in the problem. I asked the other students if there were any different answers.

DEREK: Yeah, 5 + 2 = 7. So, 2 kids walked in.

TEACHER: Can you demonstrate what you mean?

DEREK: Sure. See there are 5 kids. (Derek gets 5 kids to stand up by the door). Two kids walked in. (He gets 2 more kids and takes them out into the hall, then walks them back in the room.) Now there are 7. See? 1, 2, 3, 4, 5, 6, 7.

CLASS: Ohhhhhhhhhhh.

TEACHER: Derek, can you show us that with cubes?

Derek made a stack of 5 cubes to show the students who were first in the classroom and a stack of 2 cubes to show the students who walked in, making a total of 7.

At this time I decided to write out a number sentence for the class.

$$5 + \square = 7$$

TEACHER: Is this a number sentence for our problem?

ELLIE: Now, put the 2 in the box. That works.

ANDREW: It's like the box is holding the 2 kids that walked in.

GRADE 1, DECEMBER

I decided to present the next problem.

There are 7 kids in the classroom. Some kids left. Now there are 5 kids in the class. How many kids left the classroom?

Again, I asked the students to think about what was happening in the problem. I waited a few minutes and then reread the problem looking for a response to the question, "How many kids left the classroom?"

ALEX: 2

TEACHER: How do you know?

ALEX: If you take 7 out, there would be 0. But, when you take 2 out there would be 5 left.

TEACHER: Can you show me with cubes?

ALEX: Like, take away. OK. I have 7. Take 2 away; now I have 5 left.

TEACHER: Show me with the cubes.

Alex put 7 cubes in a tower.

ALEX: Pretend there are 2 bus kids that left the room. Now, there are 5 walkers left with you. See, take 2 away.

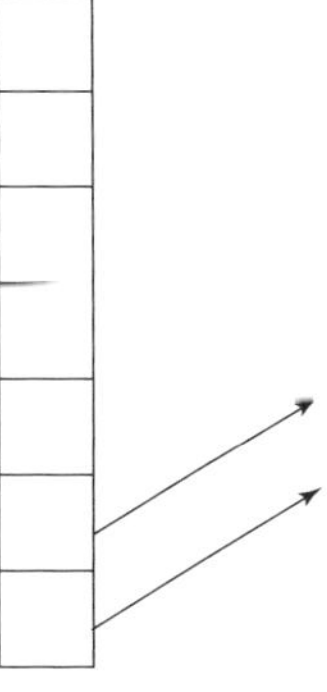

Alex took 2 cubes away and was left with this result.

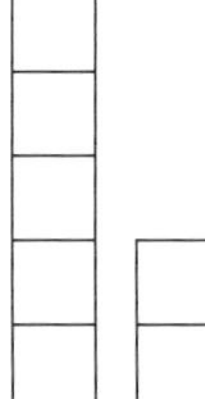

Derek stood up and pointed to himself.

TEACHER: Why are you pointing to yourself, Derek?

DEREK: I'm a bus kid. I left.

I think he was trying to make a connection to the problem.

I was very pleased to see that the cube representations from the two problems looked so similar. Although the actions to get to the end result were different, the representations still resembled each other.

I held up the two cube representations.

TEACHER: Does anyone notice anything about these cubes?

DEREK: It's the same, but on this one, 2 came in and on that one, 2 left.

ALEX: 2 came in, which gave us more. Then 2 left, so we took them away.

I was very happy that Alex was able to verbalize the actions that were taking place. My students have been having difficulty lately describing what actually happens in a given problem in context. At times, they can repeat the story to me, but they have been having trouble associating an action to the problem.

TEACHER: So, what is the same about these problems?

KAYANA: The numbers are the same.

ANDREW: Yeah, 2 came in; then 2 left. 5 were there, and 7 started there.

ALEX: $5 + 2 = 7$ and $7 - 2 = 5$. They are the same thing but turned around. See? They are the same, but the $7 - 2 = 5$ has a take away, and the $5 + 2 = 7$ has a plus.

What a great way to end a lesson! I felt very comfortable that my students recognized and understood the relationship between the two problems. I wonder if they would be able to make the same connection to a similar pair of problems that involved different numbers. I am sure they would be able to walk through the problems the way we did in this example; but would my students be able to use the connection they had already made and apply it to a new problem? I think it goes with the question, Will it *always* work? Does each addition problem have a corresponding subtraction problem? I think that is something I will explore with my students in the future.

C A S E 23

Is one acting just like zero? part 1

Alice

Grade 3, December

On our sixtieth day of school, my students identified the numbers you can count by to get to 60. Since the beginning of the year, as part of our daily routine, we have done this task for the number of days we have been in school. For more than a month, I have also recorded the multiplication sentences that matched in order to help students connect skip-counting with multiplication. Although students had seen such equations daily, on this particular day, Martha looked disturbed by the equation $1 \times 60 = 60$. Her comment, which launched a week of discussion and justification that still continues, was, "But I thought only 0 could do that!" After explaining what she meant by "do that," we were off!

Teacher: Zero does that in addition. Can you say what happens in addition when you add 0?

Martha: The number stays that number.

Teacher: And what happens in multiplication when you multiply by 0?

Marina: You just get 0.

Teacher: If I take anything times 0, I get...

Class: Zero.

Teacher: So what does 1 do in addition?

Susan: It gets 1 bigger.

Teacher: So what does 1 do in multiplication?

Todd: It gives you another of the number that you're multiplying.

Martha: I don't really understand how that could happen because how could... (Her voice trails off.)

Teacher: So, Todd, are you saying that for 60 × 1, if I add another 60, that gives me 120?

Todd: Wait. No. It keeps the number that you're using.

Martha: But, how could that happen? I thought that could only happen with 0. I thought 1 could only get you 1 more or 1 less.

Teacher: It looks as though some people have some comments for you. Call on someone.

Martha: Sharon.

Sharon: I think that it can get the same number because instead of being addition or subtraction, it's kind of saying like... if you just turn it around, like times, it's kind of saying like 1 times 60... Well, you're not really turning it around, but it gets you to...you're doing 60, one time; and 60, one time is 60. It's not 60 and another one. It's 60.

Martha: I think I'll call on Karen so she doesn't burst!

Karen: Can I draw a number sentence and show what I'm thinking? What you do is, say, I'm doing 60. What I'm doing is...if you go 1 × 60 = 60, the second number is how many 1s you have. It's not going 0 × 60 = 60, 'cause that's not adding any numbers... But 1, it shows you how many 1s you need to get to that number.

I'm not sure if Karen was noticing something about the number of 1s in any number or about the connection between thinking of one count of 60 versus 60 counts of 1.

Martha: Are you saying that... Well (big pause), I don't really get it. I don't really understand what people mean when they say "Sixty, 1 time." What does that mean?

Karen: It's just the number 60, one time.

Martha: Allison.

Allison: It's like you're adding one group of 60.

Martha: Are you saying a group of 60s, like four 60s, or are you saying one 60 group?

Alice

GRADE 3, DECEMBER

ALLISON: One 60, because 1 times 60 is 60...and it has 1 sixty times, or it has 60 one time. It's like 1, and you're counting sixty 1s.

MARINA: You know how, in two counts of 60, you have 120? Well, if you do just one count of it, it would be just 60.

SHARON: Do you get it now?

MARTHA: No.

TEACHER: Martha's wondering why is it that 1 times any number... We could be talking about *any* number here, right, Martha?

MARTHA: Right!

TEACHER: What is it about 1 when you're multiplying that always gives you back the same number? So, 1 times *any* number is always going to equal...

STUDENTS: That same number!

MARTHA: It's weird because...*that* thing, I thought, only happened with 0.

TEACHER: And it *does* happen with 0 in addition. Zero acts in addition the same way 1 acts in multiplication.

SHARON: (Very seriously spoken) This is a big question.

Next, I decided to take what felt, at the time, like a big risk. I am still not sure that this was the best timing for introducing this idea, but I wanted to see if the language and symbolism of the generalization they were wrestling with would facilitate the discussion.

TEACHER: Martha, I'm going to offer something here. It seems that Martha's question has gotten us talking about an important idea. I'm going to write what we've been talking about as a few number sentences, using the letter n to stand for *any* number, as we've done before.

I wrote n + ___ = n and n × ___ = n, and as a group, we filled in the missing numbers so that they read $n + 0 = n$, and $n \times 1 = n$.

MARTHA: My question really is, Is 1 just acting like 0 does?

TEACHER: Martha, take 0 groups of 60 markers. How many markers will you take?

MARTHA: Yeah, but you don't want to think it's 0.

CHRIS: Martha, because you start from 0. So, what's zero 60s?

MARTHA: Zero.

CHRIS: Yeah, so what's one 60?

MARTHA: Oh, 60. Ooohhh! Because I thought people were saying one group of 60s, I was thinking like 60, 60, 60. But, now I see that people were really meaning just one 60.

What I didn't realize about Martha's initial confusion, until it was revealed in the discussion in subsequent days, was that she had a way of thinking about 60×1 that caused her to see it as the 60 you already had, plus the 60 more that you get. In other words, to do 60×1, she was thinking that you already had to have the 60 to start with!

TEACHER: Are there any last comments? If you do have one, come up and let me know while everyone else gets a snack.

Many students had last comments. Sharon asked if she could write her idea on the board to explain it to Martha. Martha watched as Sharon wrote:

$$1 \times 60 = 60 + 0$$

Martha's face lit up, as she acknowledged that she understood what Sharon had written.

Martha's initial question helped reveal something that was not as obvious as it first seemed. I often find that these ideas, which experienced math learners have come to just assume, actually require some unpacking. Sometimes my assumptions have masked some important mathematical ideas at work behind what I had thought was obvious. In this case, Martha's comment led my class to critically examine the differences between multiplication and addition. I admire her ability to identify and so clearly articulate what was puzzling her. I also admire the courage she had to "go public" with her inquiry.

C A S E 24

Is one acting just like zero? part 2

Alice

GRADE 3, DECEMBER

The discussion of Martha's question also indicated to me that she had illuminated something important enough for us to examine for the next few days. I wasn't completely sure about how to manage students as they investigated the idea for themselves, but I decided to start by having them work in pairs to explore the ideas.

Partners collaborated to find a way to represent either $n + 0 = n$ or $n \times 1 = n$. Then, each pair of students shared with another pair who had worked on the other equation. During this work, there were several questions about how to represent 0 and about what 0 really is. Students called it "air" or "nothing" or a "noncounting number," because if you count by 0, you just stay on that number. Chris declared, "The lowest number you can show is 1."

Then students shared their representations with the class.

BEN: Well, me and Bob found out that 1 times 60 or 60 times 1 is sort of like saying, How much is sixty 1s?

TEACHER: 60 times 1 is the same thing as saying sixty 1s? Steven, weren't you in that group? Yesterday I heard you say something about how that works, whether the number is 12 or 40 or anything.

STEVEN: Yeah, like in that 40 you could still always find forty 1s.

MARK: Me and Daniel were saying that if you have one 10, you have just one count of it. So, like the 1 is just "one count," and so that would just be one count of 60, and one count of 60 would be just 60.

TEACHER: Can you take that idea and find a more general way of saying it? Is it true that one count of any number will always be that number?

MARK: Yes. Because it just stands for one count of it.

DANIEL: Because you're not adding anything else into it. You're just doing one count of it. You just want to do one count of it. Because if you did two counts of 10, you'd get 20, not 10.

SHARON: It's kind of cool because when you do 1 times *n*, any number, that's that number, but if you do 2 times that number, then you get that number 2 times.

Sharon seems to be noticing something that feels to her like a new way of thinking about what multiplication means. I'm not exactly sure what seems so different to her. Isn't this how we have used multiplication all along? Still, sometimes when we take a new look at some of these ideas, it does seem as though we've discovered something we never knew before! Maybe the new idea is to be able to talk about "any number."

STEVEN: (Who was absent two days ago when we had our first discussion) What's the *n* mean again?

STUDENTS: Any number.

STEVEN: Oh, yeah. OK.

CHRIS: Me and Martha figured out that 0 is the only number that you can't count to anything with...like you can't count or would just keep going 0, 0, 0, 0.

MARTHA: You wouldn't go anywhere else.

STEVEN: You're not getting anywhere else.

MARTHA: If you wanted to try that, you will probably be wasting your life.

KEVIN: It's a noncounting number.

TEACHER: What if I start at 1, and count by 0?

CLASS: You go 1, 1, 1, and 1. (Giggles)

JAMES: Isn't that Martha's theory?

TEACHER: That's part of her question.

JAMES: 'Cause like 0 is kind of like...it doesn't want any number to go ahead of itself.

STEVEN: What is Martha's question again? I wasn't here on Monday when you talked about this.

MARTHA: Well, my question is: Is 1 like 0 in times?

TEACHER: (I rephrase.) Is 1 in multiplying like 0 in adding?

STEVEN: OK, I get it now!

MARINA: The thing that's on my mind is *why* any number times 1 is still that number, and why is 0 plus any number that number? How come that works?

FRAN: I was thinking that adding 1 would be...

TEACHER: (Interrupting her too soon) We're actually not talking about adding 1...

FRAN: I know, but it has to do with why it's that. Because if you *added* 1, you wouldn't get the same number, and for multiplication, if you did it 0 times, it would just be nothing, but if you did it once, it would be that number.

TEACHER: So, Fran, are you building on the idea that Martha was noticing, that there were different numbers that did this thing in addition or multiplication? Are you trying to show why they couldn't be the same number for both, that you need two different numbers?

Fran seems to be trying to justify her hypothesis by working as if the same number could work for both operations and then showing that it can't. It seems like an elegant kind of "proof."

FRAN: Right.

TEACHER: (I refer to the sentences $n + \_\_ = n$ and $n \times \_\_ = n$.) Let's use Fran's idea. What would happen if we put the same number in the blank space?

First, we try 0 and that only works in one of the sentences. Then we try 1, and likewise, that only works in one of the sentences. Many kids "ooh" and "ahh."

TEACHER: So you're noticing something different about the way addition works from the way multiplication works. Maybe using the same number won't work because addition and multiplication operate on numbers differently.

FRAN: Right. You *have* to use different numbers.

TEACHER: Joel, you had a neat way of showing how to represent adding 0 to any number. Can you demonstrate that for us?

JOEL: (With his partner Todd) Well, we took a 10 stick, and we counted how much it was, and it was 10. Then (reaching into his pocket and pulling out nothing) here's 0, and you add it on, and you count it again, and it's still 10! So, we just added 0.

TEACHER: And would that work for any number?

STEVEN: Yeah, it's like you're putting on nothing.

TEACHER: Susan, weren't you asking yesterday about how you could represent nothing? Did Joel's representation seem to make sense as a way to show that? (She smiles and nods.)

TODD: Then we tried it with 5. We counted 5, put on 0, and counted again. We still had 5.

TEACHER: Did anyone have a way of showing what happens when you multiply times 1?

SHARON: Can I do it with my partner?

TEACHER: Sure.

SHARON: This is a 10 stick.

KAREN: (Her partner) We both did it different ways.

TEACHER: OK, show us one way first.

SHARON: (Showing the first way) This is 10. It's *ten*, 1 time. It's 10, *one* time. (She's holding up the 10 stick as she points.)

TEACHER: This reminds me of what Ben said before. Ben switched that around, and he said, "If it's 10 *one* time, then it also has to be 1 *ten* times." And he was saying that for any number you could give him, he would know how many 1s there would be in that number. Isn't it interesting to know that for any number you could think of, the number itself has that number of 1s in it?

KAREN: (Showing the second way) That's how I did it 'cause I broke the 10 stick up into ten 1s. I could do that for any number.

TEACHER: There seems to be something in this idea that offers us a way to think about what "times 1" does in multiplication.

I thought they were beginning to see that multiplication and addition are very different operations, and so we continued talking.

TEACHER: Any other thoughts or questions about Martha's question?

MARY: I don't really understand why it's not the same, like why it's not both 1 or why it's not both 0.

TEACHER: OK. Does anyone have a response for Mary? She's wondering *why* there has to be a different number in addition from the number that does that same thing in multiplication.

MARK: The reason why is that because times is different from addition, so the 1 wouldn't make sense in addition 'cause you get a different number.

TEACHER: So, what have you found out about how multiplication and addition are different? What is it about them and the way they operate on numbers that results in their needing these different numbers, 0 or 1?

FRAN: It's not like multiplication adds, or that addition multiplies! They don't do the same thing, so why *would* they use the same thing?

TEACHER: How are they different?

SHARON: This is something that's really cool. It's almost like in multiplication and addition, the set of numbers is almost totally different.

TEACHER: What do you mean?

SHARON: They really are the same numbers, but they do different things when you use them.

TEACHER: So in an addition sentence, what are you doing to these two numbers? (I point to the addends.) And in a multiplication sentence, what are you doing to those two numbers?

SAM: Well, I need some more time to think about this one.

BEN: The addition means you put this number *on top of* this number. So, I put this number on top of this number (the two addends) and I get this number (the sum).

From the gestures he is using, he seems to be talking about what would happen if you had two cube sticks, one representing each addend, and stuck the two of them together.

TEACHER: But, in multiplication?

KAREN: In multiplication, you're not sticking it on top of the other number. In multiplication, one number shows you how many times you have to plus the other number. Like in $3 \times 9 = 27$ (which she writes on the board), you don't really use 3. The 3 just tells you how many times you plus the 9.

She has written: $3 \times 9 = 27$

KAREN: The 3 shows how many times you plus it. The 9 is the number you plus. The 27 is the total amount.

SHARON: It's like 3 is the describing word, and 9 is the thing getting described.

I was ready to end the discussion with these images of what addition and multiplication are about, but Mary was eager to speak and raised a very interesting question.

MARY: If multiplication and addition need different numbers to do that, why do subtraction and division just use the same ones that addition and multiplication use? Why don't they all have different numbers? How come they just use 0 and 1 again?

TEACHER: Mary has offered us all something more to think about. Consider what we have talked about today and Mary's question for homework.

C A S E 25

Thinking about negative numbers

Carl

GRADE 7, APRIL

As I prepare a new unit on integers for my seventh-grade classes, I am curious about what my students think about negative numbers. What contexts do they think of when they see a negative number? How do they think about ordering negative and positive numbers? What understanding and skill do they have with operating on negative numbers? I decided to give my students an opportunity to tell and show me what they know. This will give me a better idea of where instruction should begin and what issues I would need to address. It will also provide an opportunity to introduce some situations, contexts, and models that might be useful as we progress with this unit.

I began the lesson by saying, "Today we are going to begin a new unit on negative numbers. Negative numbers are important because there are many things in our world that would be difficult to describe without positive and negative numbers. I am curious to find out where you see negative numbers being helpful in our world."

Here is the list that the students generated:

- Temperature: Temperatures in our world and in experiments can go below 0, so it is helpful to use the negative sign to show that a temperature is below 0.
- Money: A person can earn money and have savings, or they can have debt, so it is useful to be able to use a negative sign to show that a number represents what a person owes.
- Elevation or depth: A negative sign with a number can be used to show distance below sea level.
- Longitude and latitude: Above and below the equator.
- Taxes: When a person completes their tax form they want to know if they owe or if they will get money back. (This was a timely example because taxes were due last week.)

Carl

Grade 7, April

- Stock market: Each day the stock market can gain or lose value.
- Sports: A team or individual can gain or lose yards in football.
- Graphing on a coordinate grid: There are negative points that need to be graphed in science.

Teacher: Wow, you know of a lot of places where negative numbers can be a useful tool for representing real situations in our world. I want you to keep these contexts in the back of your mind as we move forward with this unit on negative numbers. These situations can be helpful in allowing us to sort out how negative numbers work. Before we jump into our work with negative numbers, I want you to think about positive numbers. You all know the number 9 is greater than 7. How do you know that? If I came to you and said, "I don't think 9 is greater than 7," what argument would you use to convince me that 9 is greater than the number 7?

Kerry: If you start at 1 and count up, you will get to 7 before you get to 9. (She comes up to the board and writes the counting numbers from 1 to 9 and circles 7 and 9.)

Mark: Or, you can look at it the other way with 0.

Teacher: Show us what you mean.

Mark: (Comes to the board and puts a 0 in front of the 1) 7 is closer to 0 than 9 is, so 7 is smaller.

Juan: You can show the same thing with tally marks or a graph.

| | | | | | |

| | | | | | | | |

When you match up the tally marks, that bunch of 9 has 2 tallies that cannot be matched with any from the bunch of 7. Or with a graph, 9 is taller. (He drew the following picture to show the class what he meant.)

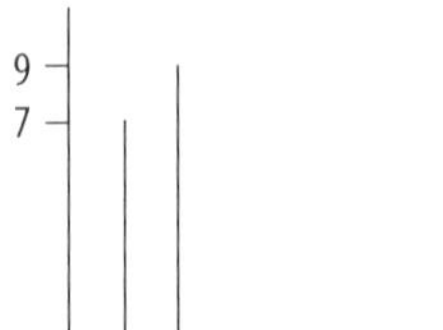

CINDY: My idea is like Juan's; 7 inches is shorter than 9 inches, or 9 cubes takes up more space than 7 cubes. $9 buys more than $7.

HEATHER: I am thinking about subtraction. $9 - 7 = 2$. This is kind of like what Juan is saying about the 2 left over. If you take 7 away from 9, then there are 2 left over.

MARION: What about addition? If you add 1 to 9, you get 10, but if you add 1 to 7, you only get 8.

HEATHER: But that means you have to know that 10 is greater than 8.

MARION: OK, well if you take a number like 4, then it takes a larger number to get from 4 to 9. $4 + 3 = 7$ and $4 + 5 = 9$.

MARK: Or, $10 - 1 = 9$ and $10 - 3 = 7$. You have to take more away from 10 to get to 7.

DANA: Well, I am thinking that division works, too. $\frac{9}{7}$ is greater than 1 and $\frac{7}{9}$ is less than 1. 7 goes completely into 9, but 9 cannot go into 7.

MINU: Mine is like Dana's. $\frac{9}{10}$ is 90% but $\frac{7}{10}$ is 70%. 90% is bigger.

SANDY: I was thinking about squares. A 9 by 9 square is 81, and a 7 by 7 square is 49. A square with sides 9 inches long is bigger than a square with sides 7 inches.

TEACHER: I know that some of you have other arguments, but now I want to change the question to include negative numbers. If we consider the numbers $^{-}9$, 7, and $^{-}7$, which of these is greater, and what is your argument to convince me? Can you use the same arguments that you have just been sharing, or do you have to come up with different arguments?

SANDY: I don't think squares work because how do you show a side length of $^{-}7$?

TEACHER: Sandy has provided us with a great example of what I am asking you to do. She took her squares argument and tried to see if she could use it to create an argument for which is greater. I am going to give you a few minutes to look at the arguments we have recorded on the board, or you can use other ones. I will give you a few minutes to think and talk in your groups.

Carl

GRADE 7, APRIL

As the groups worked on the problem, I circulated around the room and listened to their discussions. Several groups tried to use the addition, subtraction, or multiplication arguments that they had devised for 9 and 7. These groups encountered two areas of confusion.

First, they were trying to figure out how to add, subtract, or multiply negative numbers. Several students used rules they had learned previously, but most were getting their rules mixed up. For example, Heather's group "knew" a rule that "a negative and a negative make a positive." So, when adding $^{-}9 + {}^{-}7$, they got 16. Jamal's group also said that "a negative and a negative make a positive." So, for $^{-}9 - ({}^{-}7)$, they also got 16.

Then once they added, subtracted, or multiplied the numbers, they were not sure what the result indicated to them about the numbers. For example, in Heather's group, they got $^{-}9 + {}^{-}7 = 16$, and $7 + {}^{-}7 = 0$. They were not clear how the 16 and 0 helped them to make an argument about which number was greater and why.

After about 7 minutes, I called the groups back together. I decided that, initially, I did not want to get mired down in a discussion of rules when students did not have models to really help them sort out those rules. Among the groups that tried using rules, no students had connected those rules to a situation, model, or other kind of argument. They were simply rules. So, I had the groups with arguments that did not include operations share their ideas with the rest of the class first.

TEACHER: Let's start with Kerry's group. You all had an interesting conversation about Kerry's number line.

AMELIA: (She comes to the board and extends the number line that Kerry had put up in our initial discussion, now to include negative numbers, and then circles $^{-}9$, $^{-}7$, and 7.) If you are looking at positive numbers like we did earlier, then the number that is closest to 0 is smaller. If one of the numbers is positive and one is negative, then the positive is always larger. But if you look at two negative numbers, the number that is closest to 0 is bigger.

TEACHER: Can anyone explain this using a context or situation?

CINDY: We used temperature, so our number line went up and down. (She comes up and draws a vertical number line.) If it is $^{-}9$ degrees outside and the temperature warms up to $^{-}7$, then $^{-}7$ is warmer, which means it is the bigger number.

Carl

GRADE 7, APRIL

MINU: We used money. If you owe \$9, then you have less than someone who owes \$7. But, then there is a way that owing \$9 means that you owe more, so $^{-}9$ is a bigger debt.

This is an area in which contexts can be tricky. There is a way in which $^{-}9$ can be thought of as larger if the scenario is focused on the amount of debt as opposed to net worth. I was not sure how to tackle this and if it would be productive in terms of the mathematical idea of "greater than" or "less than" in the number system. So, I decided not to pursue this issue at this time. I did record it on butcher paper in case I wanted to come back to it at a later time. There is something important here about context and what we mean by larger, but I need to think about it more.

TEACHER: OK, so Amelia's group came up with three rules to sort out which number is larger. (I pointed to the three rules recorded on the butcher paper.) Do you all agree with these rules? Does anyone think they have different rules that work?

CAROLINE: I think I have one rule that works for everything. If a number is farther left on the number line, then it is smaller.

TEACHER: Interesting. Amelia, what do you think of Caroline's rule?

AMELIA: Well...it is sort of...it is sort of the same but nicer. In each of our rules, the number that is farther to the left is the one that is smaller. So, if you look at two negative numbers, the one that is closer to 0 is larger, and since it is closer to 0 the other number is to the left of it.

KERRY: You can say the same thing by saying that a number that is more right is larger.

MARION: We used Mark's subtraction idea. $2 - 9 = {}^{-}7$ and $2 - 11 = {}^{-}9$. You have to subtract more from 2 to get $^{-}9$, so $^{-}9$ is smaller.

CAROLINE: We used addition: $^{-}9 + 10 = 1$; $^{-}7 + 10 = 3$; $7 + 10 = 17$; 7 is largest because if you add the same number to each of these, 7 gets you to a bigger number.

TEACHER: How did you know that $^{-}9 + 10$ is 1?

CAROLINE: We used a number line. We started at $^{-}9$ and then went up 10. (She comes up to the number line on the board and draws a line from $^{-}9$ to 1.)

HEATHER: We tried addition, too, but it didn't help. ${}^{-}9 + {}^{-}7 = 16$ because a negative and a negative is a positive and $7 + {}^{-}7 = 0$. 16 is bigger than 0, but we don't know what that means.

I was glad that Heather brought this up now because it raised some issues that we needed to sort out. I wanted to address these issues for a few minutes so that students would have some questions in their mind for tomorrow when we move into operations with negative numbers. I thought a little confusion here might create some curiosity and help the students to understand why we are doing this work.

TEACHER: I have heard many of you using rules for thinking about negative numbers like Heather has done. Some of the rules you are using work, and some do not. Over the next few weeks, we are going to look closely at *why* some of your rules work, and others do not. To get us started, I want you to do the following problem on your own: $5 - ({}^{-}3)$.

After a few moments, I asked to hear students' answers. They shared the following possible answers: 2, ${}^{-}2$, 8, and ${}^{-}8$. I gave them a few minutes to discuss these possibilities, and then I asked for their answers again to see where we stood. Eleven students thought the answer was 2; three thought it was ${}^{-}2$; and thirteen students thought 8 was the correct answer. In their small-group discussions, I did not observe any student using a model or context to explain why they thought their answer was correct.

TEACHER: Very interesting. Over the next few weeks we are going to use models and contexts to help us sort out what is going on here. You've already mentioned some of the models and contexts, but others may be new to you. I also noticed some of you getting out your calculators. Remember, we do not only want to find the answer, but I want you to be able to explain why your answer makes sense. Can you convince me with a reasonable argument? We have 3 minutes left. I want you to write down what you think the answer is and why. This is your ticket out today.

Here are some of the responses I received for $5 - ({}^{-}3)$:

- The answer is 2 because positive numbers go to the right and negative numbers go to the left. So, if you have positive 5, then you go to the left 3 steps because you are subtracting ${}^{-}3$.

Carl

GRADE 7, APRIL

- The answer is $^{-}2$ because when a good thing happens to a bad person, that's a bad thing.
- The answer is 2 because I used a calculator.
- The answer is 2 because $^{-}3$ is the same as 3 in this case.
- The answer is 8 because with negatives if you subtract, they both turn positive.
- The answer is 8 because a positive minus a negative is a positive.
- The answer is 8 because we know that negatives cross each other out and make a positive.
- The answer is 2 because if you take a portion away from a bigger portion, you have some left over.
- The answer is 8 because when you subtract a negative from a positive, it would be just like adding the negative.
- The answer is 8 because you can't subtract a negative.
- The answer is 8 because you count up from $^{-}3$.
- The answer is 2 because you do the opposite. $5 - (^{-}3)$ becomes $5 + (^{-}3)$.
- The answer is 8 because $^{-}3$ is 3 from 0 and 5 is 5 from 0, so $3 + 5 = 8$.
- The answer is $^{-}2$ because $- (^{-}3)$ is double the minus.
- The answer is 8 because $5 - 8 = {}^{-}3$, so $5 - (^{-}3) = 8$.
- The answer is $^{-}2$ because the negative on the 3 is like a subtraction, so it lowers the number more than $5 - 3$.

It is clear that some students who got the problem correct were using rules and logic that will not hold up in all cases. Some are using logic that does hold up, but we will need to explore their reasoning more deeply. It is going to be very important for students to spend some time with a variety of models for negative numbers so they can use the model not only to help them get the correct answer but also to understand why their answer is correct. I am hoping that the models and contexts become tools to help students keep the rules straight. This has worked with other math content, so it will be interesting to see how this works with negative numbers.

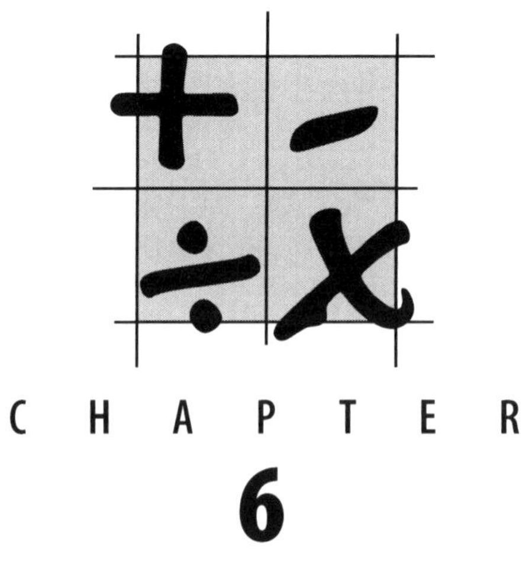

CHAPTER 6

Multiplying in Clumps

Young students who learn to think in terms of the actions of an operation know how to take the numbers apart and recombine them to perform calculations with numbers larger than the facts they hold in their head. In *Building a System of Tens* and *Making Meaning for Operations*, we saw students in action as they added, subtracted, multiplied, and divided. Implicit in all of their calculations were rules about how the operations work.

When students begin their work in multiplication, they may use several models to help them think about the operation: skip-counting, accumulating groups of equal size, and arranging items in arrays. Recalling such models when given a multiplication problem with numbers larger than they can immediately solve can help students figure out how to break the problem into parts to find the correct product. Frequently, students see how to decompose one factor, multiply "in clumps," and add up the results. This property of multiplication, in its most general form, is called the Distributive Property and is formally represented as $(a + b) \times c = (a \times c) + (b \times c)$. In the cases described in this chapter, we see students exploring this property.

At times, students keep in mind symbol patterns and lose sight of whether a particular method is actually suited to what the operation does. Specifically, there are methods that are useful for addition but need to be revised for subtraction, multiplication, or division. For example, when adding, the numbers can be broken apart by place, the components with like places added, and then those numbers can be combined to find the sum. $19 + 14 = (10 + 9) + (10 + 4) = (10 + 10) + (9 + 4) = 20 + 13 = 33$. If one is looking only at patterns of the symbols and not attending to the action of the operation, it seems as though one could do the same thing with multiplication. So, why doesn't it follow that 19×14 equals $(10 \times 10) + (9 \times 4)$ or $100 + 36$? In Case 29, Carl's students have an opportunity to explore this issue.

As you read the cases, consider the conceptual issues students confront and consider how understanding of the Distributive Property can deepen from Grade 3 to Grade 9. Case 30 also provides the opportunity to consider how the Distributive Property is applied to determine the product of two negative numbers.

Note: The error described above, which Carl's students make in Case 29, is related to one that is so common in college mathematics classes that professors have given it a name, "the freshman's dream." Elementary and middle-school teachers have the opportunity to help their students work through this error so it does not plague them in later years.

C A S E 26

Bunches of flowers

GRADE 3, MAY

Although we completed a unit on multiplication and division several months ago, we have continued to use these operations as part of our work on a daily basis. One day, we were working on a problem that I knew could be solved in various ways. I was curious about the methods my students would use and wondered if their work would help me to understand what the Distributive Property might look like to a third-grade student. What do I have to know about this property to recognize it in the work of my students? I thought a good way to start would be to ask them to solve a problem and to examine their solution strategies. Here's the problem I gave the class:

> **?** Yesterday, I found many flowers in my garden. In the morning I picked 4 bunches of flowers to give to my family. That afternoon I picked 3 more bunches to give to some friends. Each bunch had 8 flowers. How many flowers did I pick?

I wondered how the students would tackle the problem. Would I find distributivity in their work? I had structured the problem to see if some students would add the bunches together first while others would work with the morning and afternoon amounts separately and then add to find the total number of flowers. I expected they would have different approaches to the problem, and I wondered if they would see any connections among the different strategies. Would those who saw it one way be able to understand the other method as well? I also wondered if they would see ways in which thinking about solutions in this way could make solving difficult problems easier.

First, students worked on the problem individually and then they shared their ideas with a partner. While I was watching them work, I saw that some students did add the 4 and 3 and then thought about 7×8. There was also variety in how different students dealt with the multiplying and combining. Most did the 4×8 first, and then added it to the 3×8. When we came together for a whole-group discussion, students shared four ways of thinking about the problem.

LEE: I did groups of 8, and I counted them all by 2s, and I got 56. I made 8s because I picked 4 bunches in the morning and 3 bunches in the afternoon and each bunch had 8 flowers.

Lee's picture

CELIA: I got 56 as well because if you add 32 (the 4 × 8) and 24 (the 3 × 8), you get 56. First, I did 8 + 8 = 16, and then 8 + 8 + 16 = 32. 32 + 8 + 8 + 8 = 56.

ELIZABETH: I was going to do 4 × 8, but then I figured I would do 3 × 8 first. So I did 3 × 8, and I got 24. Then I went to 4 × 8, and I added another 8 to the 24 and so I got 32, and then I added 32 and 24 and it's 56.

TEACHER: Elizabeth, where are the bunches in your work?

ELIZABETH: I wasn't thinking of it as bunches. I was thinking about the morning and the afternoon.

TEACHER: So you didn't think about the 7 bunches, you thought about it as 4 bunches and then 3 bunches?

ELIZABETH: Yes, that is what the problem says.

LOUISA: I did 7 × 8. Because there are 7 bunches, and each bunch has 8 flowers.

GRADE 3, MAY

In the discussion that followed, it was pretty clear that most kids saw a connection between the two most common methods. Some had kept the two sets of bunches separate and others began by adding up the 7 bunches. Some knew there would be 7 groups of 8 but found that thinking of it as 4 groups and then 3 groups made the problem easier to solve.

Later, I asked if some students would be willing to think more about this problem, and so I met separately with this smaller group. First, I asked them to look for connections between the two different methods. They clearly saw how the different methods were similar. So I wrote $(4 \times 8) + (3 \times 8)$ and asked if anyone wanted to read it.

LAURA: Four times eight plus three times eight.

ELIZABETH: It's 32 + 24.

I asked what they would write after the equal sign, $(4 \times 8) + (3 \times 8) = \_\_\_\_\_$. Together several said 7×8. I asked why.

ELIZABETH: Because the 8 comes second.

BURT: It would just be the same because either way you still get the same number, 56.

TEACHER: The part that interests me is why can you say that $(4 \times 8) + (3 \times 8) = 7 \times 8$?

LAURA: Because the 4 and the 3 equals 7, and you take one of the 8s.

BURT: Um... I don't know. Um...I think this problem... I don't think that is what it means... because 8 + 8 is 16. Then it would be 7×16.

TEACHER: So, Burt, are you wondering... Laura said it was the 4 + 3 and one of the 8s... And, are you saying that really isn't what that means? Why do you count the 4 + 3 but not both the 8s? Is that your question?

BURT: Yeah, it would create a whole other problem. Because if you added it all together, it would be 7×16.

TEACHER: If you added all this stuff together, it would be 7×16?

BURT: And, that's not the right thing. It doesn't make sense because it is 32 + 24 in the problem.

GRADE 3, MAY

I decided to move on from here. I thought that we should look at a new problem, one for which they did not already know the answer. Would they break that new problem into smaller problems to solve it? I also wondered how they would represent their solution. I wrote 12×6 on the board and asked if they could break it up.

TEACHER: So, I've got another problem for you to think about. It seems like many people did what Laura did. She thought of the answer as 7×8, but she didn't know how much that was. So she counted two 8s and then two more 8s, until she had seven 8s. Is there a way you might think about it to pull 12×6 apart to solve it?

LINDA: That means you have to have 12 six times. I'd take two of the 12s and add them. So then I'd have 12×2, and I'd take that answer and add it two more times.

TEACHER: Could you do $(12 \times 2) + (12 \times 2) + (12 \times 2)$? Can we write it this way? Is this a true statement? $12 \times 6 = (12 \times 2) + (12 \times 2) + (12 \times 2)$.

Linda said yes, and they all agreed.

TEACHER: Why can we write it that way?

LOUISA: Because it is still six 12s, just broken up into 2 at a time and added together.

TEACHER: Is there another way we could break it up?

ELIZABETH: We can do $(12 \times 3) + (12 \times 3)$.

CATHERINE: We could also do $(12 \times 4) + (12 \times 2)$.

LAURA: $(12 \times 5) + (12 \times 1)$

TEACHER: Why can we do it all these ways?

ELIZABETH: It's like before, when we did $(8 \times 4) + (8 \times 3)$. It's still the same answer.

LAURA: It's because they all equal the same number. They are all 12×6.

TEACHER: Are you saying all of these give you 12 six times?

They all nodded. Because they had been breaking up only the 6, I wanted to see if they also thought that the 12 could be broken up.

GRADE 3, MAY

TEACHER: You've found lots of ways to break up the 6. Can we break up...

LOUISA: ...break up the 12?

TEACHER: Yes, can we break up the 12 so you would have 6 twelve times?

LOUISA: (6 × 6) + (6 × 6).

TEACHER: Does that work? How many groups of 6 do we have?

ELIZABETH: It's 6 groups of 6 and another 6 groups of 6, so it's still twelve 6s.

TEACHER: Is there another way to have 12 of the 6s?

Because time was running out, I decided to share another answer. I wrote (10 × 6) + (2 × 6) on the board.

TEACHER: What do you think of this?

BURT: It's just another way to make 12. It doesn't matter how we do it. It's still the same.

LOUISA: It's like all those other times, when we break numbers up and switch them around. The answer doesn't change because we didn't change what we had.

We had to end this conversation for the day. Do third graders use distributivity? I think so, at least from what I understand about distributivity at this point.

CASE 27

Arrays

Nicole

GRADE 4, OCTOBER

My students were working on multiplication. We were exploring a strategy of using multiplication facts we knew to find the solutions to other problems.

Nicole

GRADE 4, OCTOBER

As a class, we discussed how knowing the products of 2 × 4, 4 × 4, and 8 × 4 might help to find the solution to 12 × 4. Most students were able to do this. There were a couple of students, however, who did not understand what they were looking for. I looked for an opportunity to work with them to explore what they did and did not understand. It is the beginning of October, but I am still just getting to know some of my students as math thinkers.

Tony and Claudette had come to my attention a number of times, and their third-grade teachers had alerted me to the difficulties they encountered with math. I decided to meet with them and to use snap cubes as we looked at the relationships between the problems. First, I asked them to model a few multiplication facts using the cubes, beginning with 2 × 4. Tony started by making an "L" shape, 4 cubes high and 2 cubes wide at the bottom.

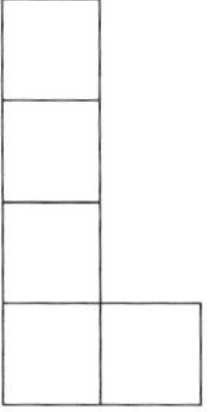

He then looked at it, puzzled. He knew it was not right, but he was stuck. Suddenly, he smiled and confidently added three more cubes to make a 2 × 4 array.

Claudette made a 3 × 5 array initially and then changed it to a 2 × 4. If they had such uncertainty about constructing an array for a number fact, how could they use the array as a model for manipulating the facts? Nevertheless I continued, hoping to get a better sense of the issues. After all, they were eventually able to construct arrays that matched 2 × 4 and were able to tell me that 2 × 4 = 8. They also recognized that a 2 × 4 array contained 8 cubes. They had some basic understanding of these arrays as models of the problem, although now I wonder if they realized that the answer to the multiplication problem and the number of cubes in the array would always be the same.

Nicole

GRADE 4, OCTOBER

Next, I had them take different color cubes and alter the array that they had made to create a 4 × 4 array. In doing this, they were able to see their original 2 × 4 array in the 4 × 4 array. I asked how they could use their 2 × 4 array to help them find the number of cubes in the 4 × 4 array. Tony started to explain how he had constructed the 4 × 4 array. Claudette understood and said, "You'd just add 8 + 8 because there are two 2 × 4 arrays here. Each one is 8, so you just add them together. 8 + 8 is 16. That's one I just know."

Tony nodded in agreement, but I knew we were on shaky ground. I decided to work backward. I had each student construct a 3 × 7 array. This time, they did it without difficulty.

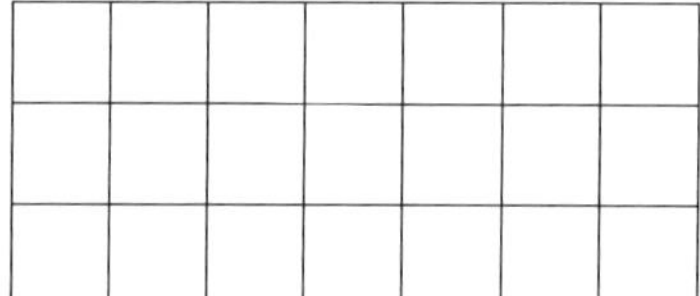

TEACHER: I know that you don't just know 3 × 7. Let's see how we can break this array into parts that you do know. Show me how you could break it into two easier parts.

They both broke their array into a 3 × 4 array and a 3 × 3 array. They told me 3 × 4 = 12 and 3 × 3 = 9. Actually, Tony skip-counted his 3 × 4 array by 3s to find the product. It was not one he "just knew," but he had a strategy for figuring it out.

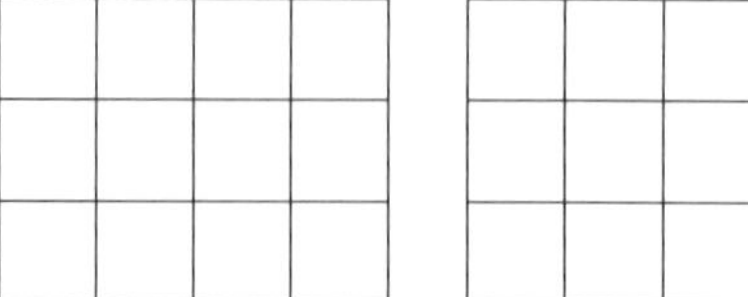

I wrote down what they had told me so far: 3 × 4 = 12; 3 × 3 = 9.

TEACHER: So, how can you use what you've already found out to help you solve 3 × 7?

Tony pushed his two smaller arrays together and said, "See, here is the 3 × 7. The 3 × 4 and the 3 × 3 make the 3 × 7."

I was pleased that he saw the connection between the smaller arrays and the original, larger array.

TEACHER: So, how would you find the answer to 3 × 7?

TONY: Easy. (He started counting the 3 × 7 array by 3s.) 3, 6, 9, 12, 15, 18, 21!

TEACHER: Good. Skip-counting by 3s would work. Now, let's try something a little different. Is there any way you could use what you know about these two smaller arrays to figure out the bigger one?

Two puzzled faces looked at the arrays and then looked back at me.

Pulling the bigger one apart again I asked, "What size is this array?" "3 × 3," they both answered confidently.

TEACHER: What does it equal?

STUDENTS: 9

TEACHER: What size is this one?

STUDENTS: 3 × 4

TEACHER: What does it equal?

STUDENTS: 12

TEACHER: So, is there any way to use these parts that you've figured out to find the answer to 3 × 7?

I pushed the two parts back together to make the 3 × 7 array. There was a long pause, but they were looking and thinking. Tony kept splitting his array into the two parts and then putting it back together again. A couple of times he skip-counted it by 3s. I pointed to the paper where I had written their information. Again, there was a long pause.

Claudette was looking at the paper. "Oh," she said. "You just add the 12 and 9 together."

Nicole

GRADE 4, OCTOBER

In the moment, I thought Claudette saw the operation of putting the two arrays back together as related to adding the two subproducts. So, what do they know? Good question! They are beginning to see the connection between pulling arrays apart and adding the subproducts. I wonder if a story problem, something with a context, might help them think about this concept. This gives me a place to start as we continue to build on the idea of using familiar multiplication problems to help solve multiplication problems involving numbers with greater values.

CASE 28

Exploring the Distributive Property

Miriam

GRADE 5, NOVEMBER

My students have been practicing solving multiplication problems independently. They know how to break down one of the numbers and multiply by the other.

For example, three different students solved 36 × 25 the following ways:

36 × 10 = 360	(36 × 20) + (36 × 5)	30 × 25 = 750
36 × 10 = 360	720 + 180	6 × 25 = 150
36 × 5 = 180		
360 + 360 + 180 = 900	900	750 + 150 = 900

I was curious to know if they would solve a story problem using the same methods as they were practicing when solving pure calculation problems. Because we were planning a bake sale, I asked the group to find the solution to the following problem:

? Eighteen students in the fifth-grade class each brought a dozen cupcakes for the bake sale. How many cupcakes did the students bring in all?

Miriam

GRADE 5, NOVEMBER

What follows is the conversation I had with one small group.

CURTIS: I skip-counted by 12 eighteen times, and my answer was 216 cupcakes.

TEACHER: How did you know that 216 was the eighteenth time?

CURTIS: On 5 times it was 60...on 10 it was 120...on 15 it was 180, and 18 was 2...no, 3 more times is 36...so 180 and 36 is 216.

ALETHEA: I drew 4 boxes and each box holds 60 cupcakes, which is 5 dozens...what 5 students brought...if all the boxes are filled that's 240 cupcakes from 20 students...since 18 is 2 less than 20, I subtracted 24, and the answer is 216.

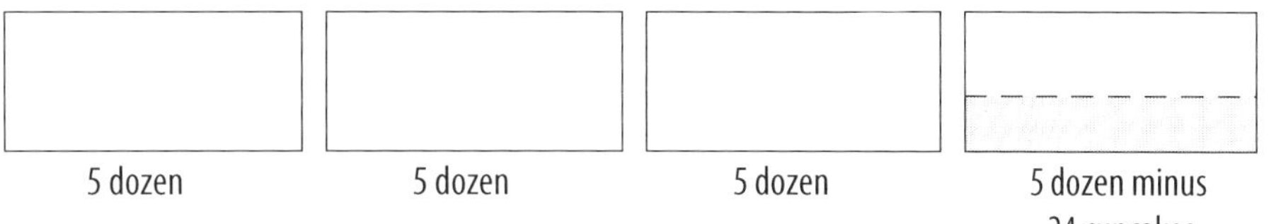

TEACHER: So what part of the fourth box was filled?

ALETHEA: 36 cupcakes...3 dozen.

TEACHER: Would Alethea have the same answer if she had added 3 dozen to 3 full boxes instead of subtracting 24 cupcakes from 4 full boxes?

LISETTE: Yes, because 15 students and 3 more students is the same as 20 − 2. They are both 18.

TEACHER: Did anyone solve it a different way?

CYNTHIA: I grouped mine by 24 nine times.
Then I grouped by 48 four times plus 24.
Then by 96 twice plus 24.
192 + 24 = 216 cupcakes.

JOHANNA: I thought 18 × 10 = 180 cupcakes and 18 × 2 = 36 cupcakes.

18 × 12 = 216 cupcakes.

TEACHER: What did Johanna do? Can anyone explain how that works?

CYNTHIA: Johanna renamed 12 and broke it down into two steps: 18 × 10 and 18 × 2.

TEACHER: Why does that work?

LISETTE: It's like the other when 18 was the same as 20 – 2.

TEACHER: So, what is Lisette saying?

CURTIS: She just said that 12 is the same as 10 and 2.

TEACHER: What does that mean when Johanna multiplied 18 by 12?

CURTIS: She multiplied 18 by 10 then 18 by 2 and added the two answers together.

TEACHER: Why does that give us the answer to 18 × 12?

THOMAS: It doesn't matter as long as you multiply 18 by 12.

TEACHER: Are you saying that I can solve the problem as long as I multiply 18 by whatever combinations of 12?

THOMAS: YES!

I brought up an item from a test I had given the class earlier. One-third of my students answered the problem incorrectly. Apparently, they had not understood the notation.

TEACHER: Can you think about the problem we had on the test? 36 × 25 = (36 × 10) + (36 × 10) + (36 × 5); tell me what that that means.

CURTIS: The 25 was changed to 10 + 10 + 5 and multiplied by 36.

TEACHER: Does everyone agree with Curtis? Why is that?

THOMAS: It's like when we said that one of the numbers can be another combination as long as it's always that number when we total it all up.

TEACHER: Can someone repeat what Thomas has said?

CYNTHIA: The 25 was changed to 10 + 10 + 5, which is 25.

TEACHER: Can you try multiplying 12 × 18 or 18 × 12 writing it out this way?

The children were eager to see how that would work.

CURTIS: It doesn't work.

TEACHER: Let's see what Curtis has done.

Curtis put his work on the board.

$(10 + 2) \times (10 + 8)$

$10 \times 10 = 100$ $\quad 2 \times 10 = 20$ $\quad 2 \times 8 = 16$

$100 + 20 + 16 = 136$

TEACHER: Did Curtis multiply 12×18?

ALETHEA: He multiplied 2×18 but only 10×10. He forgot 10×8.

LISETTE: So, $10 \times 8 = 80$, and $136 + 80 = 216$. That works!

TEACHER: Curtis, do you know why your answer was incomplete?

CURTIS: I didn't use all my numbers for 10×18.

JOHANNA: I tried $(10 + 2) \times (9 + 9)$ for 12×18.

$10 \times 9 = 90$

$10 \times 9 = 90$ $\quad 90 + 90 + 18 + 18 = 216$

$2 \times 9 = 18$

$2 \times 9 = 18$

TEACHER: We have found many ways to solve this story problem. What have we concluded?

THOMAS: We can solve a multiplication problem with skip-counting by one of the numbers that many times as the other number.

LISETTE: It's a good idea to break down a number to make it easier to find the answer.

CYNTHIA: You have to make sure that when you name a number you multiply all the smaller numbers by the other number.

JOHANNA: It doesn't matter what you rename the number as long as they equal the number.

CURTIS: Make sure you use up all your numbers before you add them up.

Miriam

GRADE 5, NOVEMBER

ALETHEA: You don't have to draw the pictures all the time to show what you mean.

TEACHER: So, you mean to tell me that you can solve any problem by renaming the numbers? Then try 24 × 25.

Curtis was the first one to share (10 + 10 + 4) × (10 + 10 + 5)

10 × 10	10 × 10	10 × 5
10 × 10	10 × 10	10 × 5
4 × 10	4 × 10	4 × 5

TEACHER: Curtis broke apart both factors into three parts. I'd like you to draw a picture or use a different method to see if he found all the parts he needs to multiply.

I was very satisfied with the students' responses. I know that they enjoy working in small groups. They are not apprehensive about the sharing of ideas, and they are really listening to each other and adding their own thinking to the conversation. I am also noticing that they use the down time to think an idea through. This is something that I have been stressing, and it is working better. I do hope that now, with practice, they will think about breaking down numbers to help them when they have to solve problems using numbers with greater values.

CASE 29

Picturing the Distributive Property

Carl

GRADES 7–9, NOVEMBER

While planning for a session to review the Distributive Property, I realized this could provide an excellent opportunity for students to continue to use their growing expertise with representations. I wanted them to figure out why the Distributive Property works and to create arguments for why they know it will work for all numbers. However, as I planned, I became concerned that I was setting students up to answer a question that they did not really have. I was going to ask them to make sense of the Distributive Property when they thought they already understood it. Because most of my students are proficient at doing the calculations involved with the Distributive Property, I expected I would hear the same comments as students have made in past years. "We already know how to do this." "Why are we doing this?" I realized that I needed to challenge their understanding of the Distributive Property and stimulate their interest in thinking about it further.

I wanted to develop a scenario related to the concepts we are studying, requiring students to make sense of something that is puzzling to them. I have found this strategy to be a great way to generate questions in their minds and prepare them to explore familiar ideas more deeply. So, how could I raise the challenge? Students clearly know that $4(3 + 5) - (4 \times 3) + (4 \times 5)$, but do they know how to apply the Distributive Property to $(4 + 7)(3 + 5)$? Aha! Here is a challenge for them. I like the idea of students working on this problem because it will raise the level of thinking required. It will also lay a foundation for our continued work with the Distributive Property later in the year when they are asked to multiply $(x + 9)(x + 4)$.

So, I have the challenge, but now I need an engaging situation in which to place this challenge. One way to think of $(4 + 7)(3 + 5)$ is in the context of finding the area of a rectangle with a length of $(4 + 7)$ units and a width of $(3 + 5)$ units. I also find that if I put students in a situation of employment in which their boss wants them to figure something out, they are more eager to take on the challenge. They have a "real" audience. So, here is what I came up with:

THE GARAGE PROBLEM

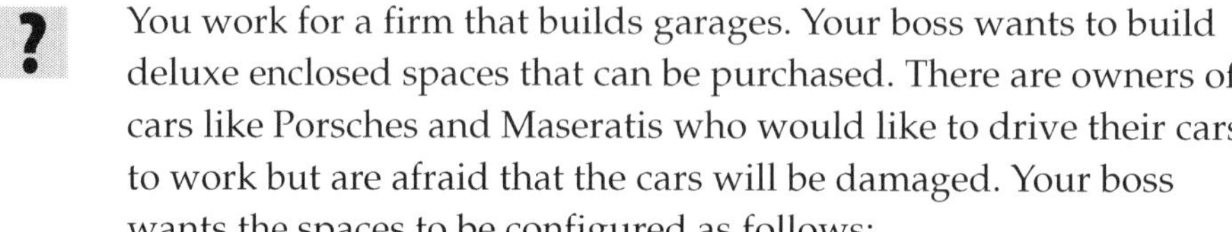

You work for a firm that builds garages. Your boss wants to build deluxe enclosed spaces that can be purchased. There are owners of cars like Porsches and Maseratis who would like to drive their cars to work but are afraid that the cars will be damaged. Your boss wants the spaces to be configured as follows:

The length of the garage is 9 feet longer than the width of the owner's car. The width of the garage is 4 feet longer than the width of the owner's car.

So, you represent the dimensions using variables:

Length: $w + 9$ Width: $w + 4$ (w is the width of the car in feet.)

The garage will have special flooring. To determine the amount of flooring that is needed, you must multiply the dimensions of the space. You show the following expression to your boss and tell him that all he has to do is substitute the width of a car for w and he will have the area. Your boss asks, "What's another way to write $(w + 9)(w + 4)$ if we don't know the width?" What would you tell him? How can you check to see if you are correct?

I begin class by telling the students that we are going to review and extend their understanding of the Distributive Property. We practice with a couple of items such as $3(7 + 4)$ and $6(x + 2)$. Most students have no problem working through the procedure. Then I give them the garage problem. After about 10 minutes of discussion in their small groups, we discuss what they have come up with.

JOSH: We think it is $w^2 + 36$. You need to multiply the w's and the 9 and 4.

KIM: But we think that it is $2w + 36$ because you have 2 w's.

JOSH: We thought that at first, but $w \times w$ is not $2w$. Like 10×10 is not 2×10, which is 20; it is 100, which is 10^2.

TEACHER: What do the rest of you think of Josh's thinking?

Jeremy: I agree with Josh. It's like what we talked about a while ago. Something to a power is that number multiplied the number of times the little number is. It is not $2 \times w$ but $w \times w$.

Teacher: OK. Josh seems to have a strong argument using a contradiction to show that $w \times w$ is not $2 \times w$. So, what about Josh's team's idea? Do you agree with $w^2 + 36$, or does someone have a different proposal? (Students either agree with Josh or are not sure.) So, how can we check this? Did anybody have a way to check this?

Sandy: You could do what Josh just did and try the number 10 for w. 10×10 is $100 + 36$ is 136. Is 136 right? I'm not sure what to do now.

Jamal: You need to go back to the original problem. $10 + 9$ is 19 and $10 + 4$ is 14. So, 19×14 is (he gets out his calculator) is 266. It doesn't work.

Teacher: I am going to give you 2 minutes in your groups to explain why Jamal thinks this does not work. Then, if you agree, can you come up with another idea for what $(w + 9)(w + 4)$ equals?

The groups are fairly clear about Jamal's use of a counterexample but do not seem to have any new ideas for the scenario problem. I think my plan has worked. They are curious and are in a position to want to revisit the Distributive Property. They now have a question in their own minds.

Teacher: So, Sandy and Jamal have generated a counterexample: If $w = 10$, then Josh's method gives us 136, but the original expression gives us 266. Does anyone have a new conjecture or proposal? (The class is quiet.) OK, right now we don't have everything we need to make sense of this situation. One important tool for understanding this is the Distributive Property. So, for the rest of this period we need to go back and extend our understanding of this property. Then tonight for your homework, I want you to use the ideas and representations that we will work with to see if you can come up with an answer to the scenario problem that works.

I write the problem 19×4 on the board.

Carl

GRADES 7–9, NOVEMBER

TEACHER: One way to mentally calculate 19 × 4 is to decompose 19 into 10 + 9 and then compute (10 + 9)4, which, using the Distributive Property, is (10 × 4) + (9 × 4). At the beginning of the year, we took a close look at what multiplication means and reviewed different representations that we could use to show multiplication. What were some of those ideas and representations?

Students respond with two ideas: arrays and groups of equal size. I then give them 15 minutes to work in groups to create at least two different ways to show that (19 × 4) = (10 × 4) + (9 × 4). I say they can use story contexts, diagrams, arrays, and other ideas about multiplication.

As I listen to the groups' discussions, I identify at least six different strategies that can be used when thinking about the relationships. I choose groups to share in a particular order, intending that students will make some connections between each of the approaches. I then want to see if they can generalize any of these arguments.

Strategy 1: Chandler writes on the board:

$$(19 + 19 + 19 + 19) = (10 + 9) + (10 + 9) + (10 + 9) + (10 + 9) =$$
$$(10 + 10 + 10 + 10) + (9 + 9 + 9 + 9) = (10 \times 4) + (9 \times 4)$$

Strategy 2: Sam writes:

```
10 + 10 + 10 + 10
 9 +  9 +  9 +  9
 |    |    |    |
 ↓    ↓    ↓    ↓
19 + 19 + 19 + 19
```

SAM: If you look just at the top two rows, you can see 4 × 10 and 4 × 9. If you look at the bottom row, it's 4 × 19.

Strategy 3: Henry draws a picture and explains, "4 groups of 19 is the same as 4 groups of 10 and 4 groups of 9."

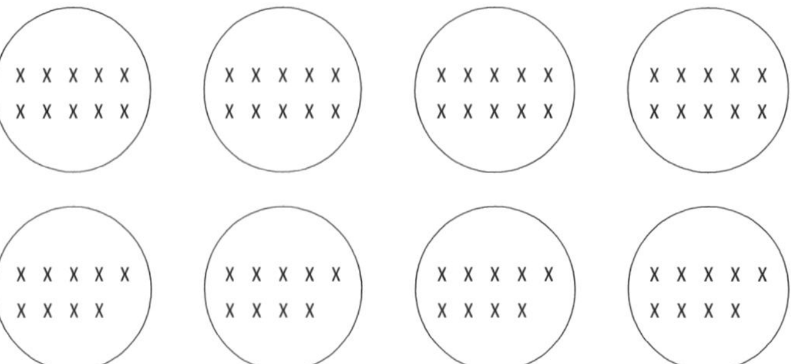

Strategy 4: Elizabeth draws an array.

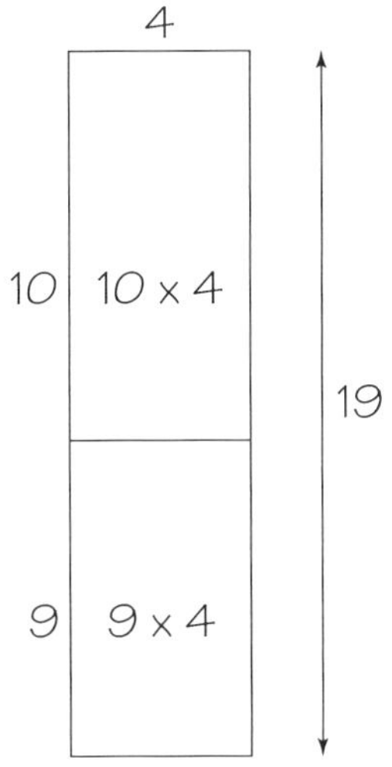

Elizabeth: A 19 by 4 array can be broken into 10 by 4 and 9 by 4 arrays. They are the same because they have the same area.

Strategy 5: Gwen presents a similar diagram but describes it as 19 rows of 4 cookies.

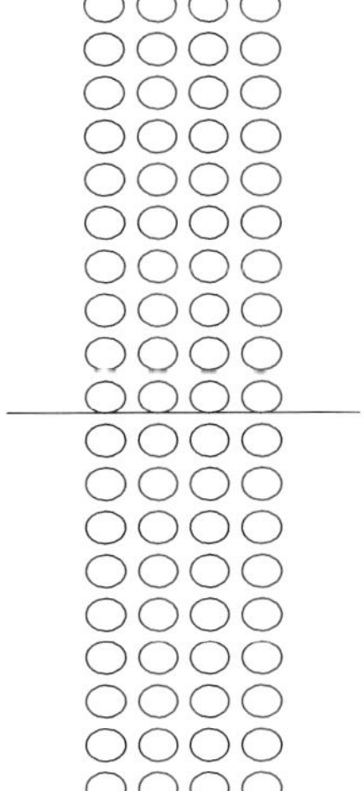

Strategy 6: Jamie presents a story context.

Jamie: 19 people with 4 tickets is the same as 10 people having 4 tickets and 9 people having 4 tickets.

Now that we have all of these representations to consider, I ask the class what connections they see between them.

CHANDLER: They all kind of show the same thing—that 19 four times is the same as 10 four times and 9 four times.

JAMIE: Gwen's diagram shows my 19 people with 4 tickets in an organized way except you would need to change the cookies to tickets. You are just breaking the group into two groups that still have the same number of things. The people and tickets do not change.

SIMONE: I have a different story and diagram to go with it, but it does not look the same. Bob buys 4 boxes of doughnuts with 19 inside each box. Larry buys 4 boxes of doughnuts with 10 in each box and 9 boxes of doughnuts with 4 doughnuts in each box. (Simone then draws the following.)

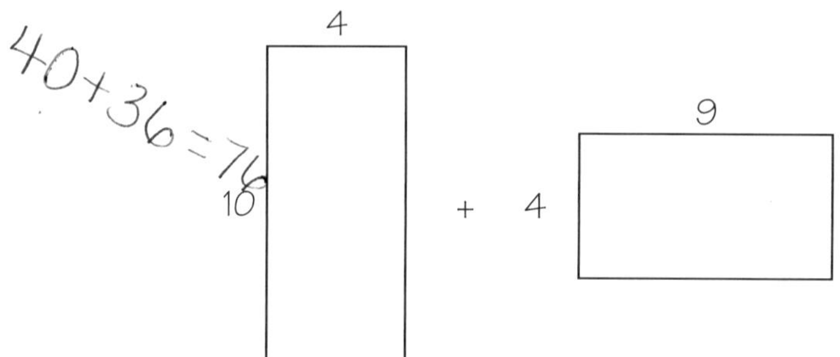

TEACHER: So, does this give us the same answer? (Students get out their calculators and punch in 10 × 4 and 4 × 9. They are all indicating that the answer is correct.) OK, so we are getting the correct answer, but there is something that feels different about Simone's story and Jamie's story. Are these the same or different, and does it matter?

Students are quiet for a while, and then Josh speaks up.

JOSH: In Jamie's story the 19 is people and the 19 is split into 10 and 9. With Simone's story, the 19 starts out as doughnuts, but with Larry there are 10 doughnuts and 9 boxes.

Time is running out for the class period, and I am unsure what issues Simone's story and diagram are raising. She starts with 4 boxes, each with

19 donuts, and compares that to 14 boxes with different amounts in them. I am not sure if students will see this nuance or if it will even be helpful. I decide to move forward with my agenda and take some time to think this over.

TEACHER: So, does this matter? We do not have time to sort this out now, but we have gotten far enough for you to do the homework tonight. You have two tasks: 1) You have a friend who thinks that you just got lucky with (19 × 4) = (10 × 4) + (9 × 4). Your friend does not think this will work for other numbers. Take one of these arguments, and see if you can use it or modify it to show your friend why this Distributive Property will work for *any* numbers. 2) See if you can use one of these arguments to show why (10 + 9)(10 + 4) does not equal 10 × 10 + 9 × 4.

SUMMARY OF HOMEWORK

Student arguments for why the Distributive Property works for any numbers:

1. Most students presented one other instance of the Distributive Property, such as 39 × 5 = (34 × 5) + (5 × 5). Many used one of the representations to show why the new example works.
2. A few students restated the Distributive Property using letters such as $a(b + c) = ab + ac$ but did not explain why this always works.
3. A number of students used explanations like Margaret's: "It will always work because you are only splitting the number into two separate groups. If you add them back together, you will always get the same number. Every number can be broken into parts. Breaking the number, multiplying each, and adding them back together is the same as just multiplying the original number."
4. Tim's writing was also typical and seemed to be a verbal restatement of the Distributive Property: "It will always work because it is multiplication. You can always break one number up and multiply the two new numbers by the second and get the same answer."
5. Kiah wrote: "$(a)(b) = z$; $a = x + y$; $(x + y)(b) = z$"

Student arguments for what (10 + 9)(10 + 4) equals:

1. Most students could show that this multiplication did not equal 100 + 36, but they could not come up with a way to show what would be multiplied to get the correct answer and why.

Carl

GRADES 7–9, NOVEMBER

2. Caitlin: "Mary picked 10 flowers in the morning and 4 flowers in the evening. She did this for the last 10 days of October and the first 9 days of November. In all Mary picked 266 flowers." Caitlin did not have an arithmetic sentence to match this.

3. A couple of students drew arrays or rectangles, but they would count the number of squares to show that it was 266 and not 136.

4. Audrey, Christina, and Alexis each used the traditional algorithm for multiplication to show what needed to be multiplied, but they did not explain why these parts needed to be multiplied.

$$\begin{array}{r} 19 \\ \underline{\times\ 14} \end{array}$$

"To do this multiplication, you do 4 × 9, 4 × 10, 10 × 9, and 10 × 10."

5. Susan created the following diagram:

14

19

10 x 10	10 x 4
9 x 10	9 x 4

6. Edgar:

$x(a + b) = xa + xb$
$y(a + b) = ya + yb$
So $(x + y)(a + b) = (xa + xb + ya + yb)$

C A S E 30

Multiplying negative numbers

Carl

Grades 7–9, October

Typically, an algebra course focuses on negative numbers early in the year because it is hard to go very far without running up against negative numbers. They are important when simplifying expressions and solving equations, and of course, they surface when working with the coordinate system. As I looked through the textbook, I wanted students to have more than a bunch of memorized rules for integers. I wanted them to have contexts and models they could use to help them sort out what happens when we operate on negative numbers. I also wanted to deepen their thinking about what different operations mean so they could use these insights about operations to assist them in creating arguments and justifications.

Initially, we began by looking at different contexts and models in which negative numbers surface. Students generated the following list: temperature, number lines, movement of elevators, sports, sea level, and debt. I also introduced them to two other models: 1) the charged particle model: Think of a beaker of positively and negatively charged particles. When one positively charged particle is combined with one negatively charge particle, the net result is a 0 charge. So 4 positively charge particles combined with 7 negatively charged particles results in a charge of $^{-}3$. 2) Hot air balloon: Each blast of hot air (representing $^{+}1$) raises the balloon 1 foot and each additional sandbag (representing $^{-}1$) lowers the balloon 1 foot. Each time the balloon vents hot air, it drops 1 foot, and each time a sandbag is dropped over the edge of the basket, the balloon rises 1 foot. Because we are flying over Death Valley, the balloon can go below sea level.

Armed with these contexts and models, students spent several lessons trying to make sense of what happens when we add and subtract integers and creating arguments to support their thinking. For example, to explain why subtracting a negative is the same as adding a positive, a number of students used the taking away of debt, the taking away of sandbags, or the taking away of negatively charged particles to show that the net result is an increase in value or height. Students could also describe what happens when a positive number is multiplied by a negative number. For example, 3 times a debt of \$4 is an example of $3 \times (^-4)$, which results in $^-12$, or a debt of \$12. I was feeling good about their work and the thinking that they were doing, so I decided to give them a challenge for homework. "What happens when you multiply a negative number times a negative number? Create an argument to explain why this is always true."

Students came up with different kinds of arguments. Some arguments were really just restatements of the question itself, such as "Negative signs cancel each other out. When negative signs come together they equal a positive. So $^-4 \times {}^-6 = 4 \times 6 = 24$." Some students used the idea of inverses: "If you multiply 1 times any number, it will be the same number. So if you multiply $^-1$ times any number, it will be the opposite. So $^-1 \times {}^-5 = 5$. The same is true for any negative number. A negative would be that many times the other negative only the opposite."

Nadir and Cindy called upon the models we had used to explore negative numbers.

NADIR: If I received 3 bills in the mail each worth \$5, then I owe \$15, which is a negative 15. But if my mom says, "You do not have to pay those bills, I will," then she has removed 3 bills worth \$5 each. This is $^-3 \times {}^-5$, which is a \$15 gain for me.

CINDY: If I throw 4 groups of 5 sandbags over the edge of the basket, the balloon will rise 20 feet. This is the same as $^-4 \times {}^-5 = 20$. The first factor is the number of groups thrown out, and the second factor is the number of sandbags in each group.

I feel these kinds of arguments reveal a strong understanding about negative numbers and multiplication. The models Nadir and Cindy used are based on the idea that multiplication means "groups of equal-sized groups." Their scenarios represent both negative numbers and also an action associated with multiplication.

Ian cited the Internet encyclopedia, *Wikipedia*, as the source for his argument.

Ian's argument starts with the idea that $0 \times n$ must equal 0.

Let $n = {}^-4$ and replace 0 by $(3 + {}^-3)$. This results in $(3 + {}^-3) \times (^-4) = 0$.

If we use the Distributive Property on the left side, we arrive at

$$(3 + {}^-3) \times (^-4) = (3 \times {}^-4) + (^-3 \times {}^-4).$$

Therefore, $(3 \times {}^-4) + (^-3 \times {}^-4)$ has to equal 0.

Because we already know $(3 \times {}^{-}4) = ({}^{-}12)$, then $({}^{-}3 \times {}^{-}4)$ must equal 12.

Ian's argument relies on the consistency of the number system. If we apply what we know about multiplying by 0, the Distributive Property, and additive inverses, then $({}^{-}3 \times {}^{-}4) = 12$. Although he has offered a demonstration with particular numbers, the argument will work with any pair of negative numbers.

As I look at their arguments, I am impressed with the way these students are trying to use what they know about numbers, vocabulary terms, and operations to come up with a logical explanation of why a negative number times a negative number results in a positive number. I am left with questions about how students make sense of the more formal mathematical proofs based on systematic logic and the coherence of a number system, like the argument Ian presented. What relevance and value do they see in this kind of argumentation? Clearly, we (my students and I) have a long way to go in this regard. However, students are definitely energized by this "thinking" process, and they have become much clearer about how operations behave with different classes of numbers. I think this will be of great benefit to them as we move into more abstraction with algebra. I will be curious to hear their responses to each other's arguments. Which ones do they find compelling or not and why?

CHAPTER 7

Exploring Rules for Factors

In Alice's classroom, students begin each day by looking at the number of days they have been in school. Then they identify the factors of that number, or in the words of some third-grade students, "the numbers you can *count by* and land on the number of the day." This daily routine generates considerable curiosity, and after some time, students start generating conjectures for rules that govern the patterns they notice. However, once they have generated a rule, there are several questions to consider: Does this rule always work? If so, how can this be proved? If this rule does not always work, what are the exceptions, and why?

When Jean's fourth-grade students were studying the factors of the multiples of 100, their investigations led them to similar questions: Is every factor of 100 also a factor of *all* multiples of 100? Again, how can students prove this?

In the fifth-and-sixth-grade class that Rosalie observed, students addressed another question: If two numbers are factors of a third number, is their product also a factor of that third number? When they realized the answer is "sometimes," they wanted to find out for what numbers the statement is true.

As you read these cases, identify the generalizations students articulate, and then consider those same questions for yourself.

CASE 31

Factors of factors, part 1

Alice

GRADE 3, MARCH

Each morning, we look at the number of days we have been in school. We then determine what numbers we can count by to get to that "Days in School" number. Over the course of the year, we have been collecting these data and posting them on one wall of the classroom. For example, one section of the wall looks like this:

18	19	20	21	22
1	1	1	1	1
2	19	2	3	2
3		4	7	11
6		5	21	22
9		10		
18		20		

Once we came to our study of factors, I told my class that, in this activity, we had been finding the factors of the Days in School number. By this time in the school year, students have noticed many things about factors, and they seem rather comfortable about offering comments like these:

- If 4 is a factor, then 2 has to be a factor.
- If 10 is a factor, then 5 is a factor, too.

Alice

GRADE 3, MARCH

- If 3 isn't a factor, then 6 can't be and 9 can't be.
- I think today's number won't have very many factors because yesterday's number had so many. Yesterday's number took all the factors.
- Anything that 20 will go into, 4 has to go into.

My students have even expanded these generalizations into such statements as:

- If there is an even number of 2s (i.e., if I can jump by 2 an even number of times), then 4 has to be a factor. If there's an odd number of 2s, then 4 can't be a factor.
- If there is an even number of 3s (i.e., if there is an even number of jumps of 3), then 6 has to be a factor. If there's an odd number of 3s, then 6 can't be a factor.
- If there is an even number of 5s (if there is an even number of jumps of 5), then 10 has to be a factor. If there's an odd number of 5s, then 10 can't be a factor.

Recently in our mathematics lessons, we have been examining the factors of 300 by building on what students know about the factors of 100. For instance, because students know that there are five 20s in 100, they know there are ten 20s in 200, and fifteen 20s in 300. After a few days of this work, I asked students to say which one of the following statements they believed to be true:

1. All of the factors of 100 are also factors of 300.
2. Most of the factors of 100 are also factors of 300.
3. Some of the factors of 100 are also factors of 300.

When I asked students to explain their thinking, the few students who chose 2 or 3 said they couldn't exactly say *all* because they hadn't tried them *all.* (Although, as a group, we had!) Ben had a different idea. He said, "It has to be *all* because it's like the things we've noticed every morning with our Days in School chart. It's like when you play solitaire. When you move the card on the bottom over, all the cards on top of it go with it. It's like that with factors. When a number goes over to be a factor of another number, it takes all of its factors with it to be factors of that other number. It has to work." Ben's solitaire model was often referenced by students as they offered explanations for how they knew certain factors of one number were also factors of its multiples.

Alice

GRADE 3, MARCH

Because so many ideas about factors seemed to be converging at once, I decided to use this as an opportunity to further explore an idea that my students seemed to be using informally already: If n is a factor of m, then all the factors of n are also factors of m. Although I wasn't sure how to structure the exploration, the time had come for my class to examine this generalization more closely.

I decided to have students work in pairs with a number that was interesting to study and yet manageable for them. I chose the number 48 for the whole class to use. We began by listing the factors of 48, and then I asked them to choose a factor of 48, and see if all the factors of that factor were also factors of 48. I wrote on the chart:

"Is it true that all the factors of ___ are also factors of 48?"

We substituted each factor we had listed on the chart into the blank in this statement, just to hear what it would sound like. Students giggled when they heard how the statement sounded when some of the factors were inserted in the blanks. We decided that for a few of the factors, the statement seemed a bit too obvious. Because some factors only had one, two, or three factors, and those factors were clearly also factors of 48, we eliminated them as choices to explore. The factors we eliminated were 1, 2, 3, 4, and 48.

Martha asked how you would know if it was true or not. "But how could you show it?" I said that was exactly what we were going to work on today. Steven asked, "Is this like the solitaire thing again?" I said that was part of what inspired this. I asked, "Is it true that the factors of numbers carry all their factors with them?"

Before students got started, Mary said, "You can't really switch it around, though. We're saying the factors of the factors of 48 are also factors of 48, but we're not saying it the other way around. We're *not* saying all the factors of 48 are factors of every factor of 48, right?" Although everyone agreed with Mary's caveat, it would turn out that this was a difficult idea for students to hold onto as they worked through their explorations, especially with 16 as a factor of 48.

Students joined with their partners and decided which factor of 48 they would try first. Many pairs opted to use snap cubes to help with their investigation. Most took enough snap cubes to make the factor they were working on, but surprisingly, did not take 48 cubes. I wanted to highlight this point, so I said, "I'm hearing many partner groups trying to figure out how many cubes to take. It seems that one of the first decisions you and your partner will have to make is how many cubes you will need to take. Do you need all 48 cubes, or do you just need enough cubes to match the number you're working on as a factor?"

Within the first few minutes, many groups realized that they needed all 48 cubes. Most groups thought about it in the same way that Mary explained it to her partner, "First, let's find all the factors of 16. If we can find all of them, then we could test them on 48." Interestingly, no one took *more than* 48 cubes. (I had thought some pairs might take 48 *plus* the number of cubes they would need for the factor they were working on.) Some pairs that were exploring the factors of 24 (as factors of 48) only took 24 cubes because they recognized that if a factor worked for 24, they could just double it for 48.

After working for 15 minutes, I gathered the class to hear how things were going so far. I wanted students to share those first decisions with each other. Fran and Holly showed how they began exploring whether or not all the factors of 24 were also factors of 48. Each one of them had taken 24 cubes to work with the factors. They explained that one of them would try a potential factor of 24. If it "worked," then the other girl would put her cubes into those groups, and then they could see how it would work for 48. Their solution appealed to many students, but most thought you could only do it with 24 because it was half of 48. Mary thought you might be able to do it with other factors "if you had more people in a group working together."

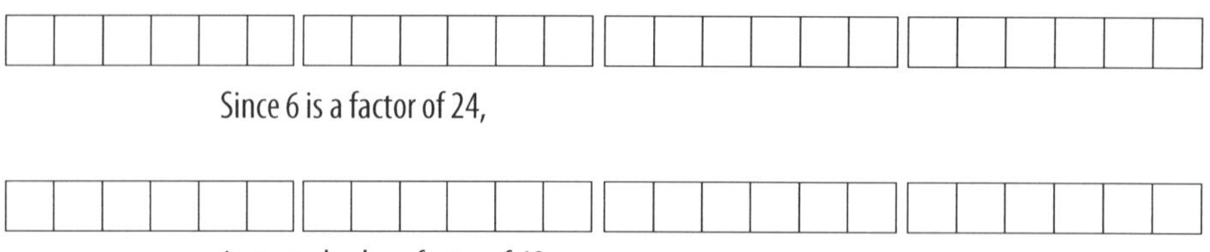

The next day, students continued working on testing the factors of 48, to see if all the factors of the factors were also factors of 48. When we gathered to share our results, students brought their cubes and their recording sheets to the rug. Many groups created lists of factors of the factors they were working on. Then they systematically tested each one of those to see if it was also a factor of 48. If the factor "passed the test," students would circle, check, or record it on their papers. In this way, the students kept track of their trials and also maintained a record of their results.

Sharon and Karen's work shows how they recorded their results and then revised them for use during the sharing session. As Sharon explained, "I wanted to show the gaps where there was a factor of 48 that wasn't a factor of 24. I thought it would be confusing for people to see the 24 over the 16. They might think it didn't match, but it does. It's just that the 16 doesn't work for 24; but all of 24's factors are also factors of 48. We tried them all." (As these girls were working, they thought they had discovered an exception. When they noticed 16 is not a factor of 24, they came rushing over to say the "rule" didn't work. Chris reminded them that we weren't talking about the switch-around of it, just the other way. When Sharon and Karen prepared their results for the group discussion, they were careful not to mislead others!)

factors
(1,2,3,4,6,8,12,24)
(1,2,3,4,6,8,12,24)
Works
Accuritt!
no 16 in 24
no 48 in 24
(1,2,3,4,6,8,12, 24)
(1,2,3,4,6,8,12,16,24,48)
Sharon and Karen

Marina and Susan built on the idea presented by Fran and Holly the day before. To explore whether or not all the factors of 16 were also factors of 48, they made three "sticks" of 16 cubes each. In this way, each of them could have a stick, and then they would see if they could break up the third stick. They said they decided to do it this way because it would be fairer than having one person work with 32 cubes and the other person work with 16 cubes.

Susan explained, "We tried the factor 16. Then we tried its factors like this. Let's say we tried 8. I broke my stick up into 8s, then Marina broke hers into 8s, then we tried the third stick. If we could break it up into 8s, then we knew 8 worked."

Many students were bothered by this explanation. Martha questioned why they were using 48 when they were supposed to be finding out about 16. Other students indicated that they, too, were confused by that part.

After much questioning and explaining, I mentioned that the class seemed bothered by the way the girls were testing out factors of 16 while they were also testing out factors of 48. I asked if they could first show us what they found out about the factors of 16, and then carry it out to show the factors of 48.

Susan repeated the process using a different factor of 16, 4. She broke her 16-stick into 4s and declared that this showed that 4 is a factor of 16. Then Marina broke her 16-stick into 4s and then they broke the last 16-stick into 4s. Wow! Although it took the class a while to accept their strategy of simultaneously testing the factors of factors, and the factors of the multiple itself, the demonstration offered a convincing argument.

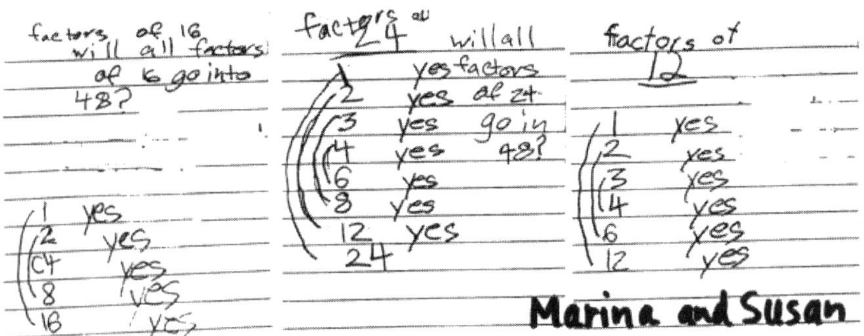

As the discussion drew to a close, the class seemed certain that it was, indeed, true that all the factors of the factors of 48 were also factors of 48. I asked them if they thought this was something special about the number 48 or if they thought it was true of all numbers. Somebody suggested we try a prime number like 53. We substituted 53 into the statement, which became, "Is it true that all the factors of 1 are also factors of 53?" and "Is it true that all the factors of 53 are also factors of 53?" It worked! Still, I wanted to push them to consider if this would always work.

Alice

GRADE 3, MARCH

The next day I told the class that I kept wondering about something. "Is this something special about only some numbers, or is it true for any number and its factors?" I asked what it would take for them to know whether this conjecture under investigation would always hold up.

SUSAN: I think it works on all numbers because I think it's like what we keep saying about our chart. We keep saying every other 2 is a count of 4. Well, since 4 is a factor, 2 has to be a factor. We keep saying that over and over.

TEACHER: That's exactly why we're investigating this. We're saying it over and over, but do we really believe it, or are we just used to saying it?

SUSAN: I believe it because it's like what we say with 5 and 10.

MARTHA: I have a way of proving that it works.

TEACHER: For all numbers?

MARTHA: If 4 is a factor, then 2 has to be a factor. 2 is a factor of 4. They sort of like have to go together.

MARY: If it's a multiple of that number, then its factors go with it to that multiple.

CHRIS: I have an example. If you're using 8, then 4 is a factor of 8 and all of 4's factors go with it to 8.

TEACHER: Is that only true for numbers like 4 and 8, though?

MARINA: This reminds me of Ben's idea of solitaire.

TEACHER: How so?

MARINA: Because the factor's numbers carry onto it. Like what Chris was using. 16 is a multiple of 8, so all of 8's factors get carried to be factors of 16, too.

BOB: I think it only works for those special numbers that you can keep breaking down by splitting in half.

TEACHER: So does this only work for special numbers like that?

MANY: No.

Alice

GRADE 3, MARCH

At this point, we tried some numbers that were suggested by students. We tested our conjecture with 25 and 80. Students agreed that the rule worked for these numbers. I asked how many numbers we would have to try before we were convinced that the rule always worked.

SUSAN: One or two more.

TEACHER: Would that be enough to convince us that it's always true?

MANY: No.

TEACHER: Then what could we do to be sure whether this would always work or not?

MARK: Try a really high number.

TEACHER: If we tried a really high number and it worked, would that really convince you?

MARK: No.

MARY: I was just thinking if we could find one that doesn't work, then we'd know, but I can't think of one that doesn't work.

TEACHER: So if we found an exception...

MARK: I was thinking that...well, maybe prime numbers. No, we already know those work. Maybe there's an odd number that wouldn't work.

KAREN: I have two things to say. I think that all prime numbers would work.

DANIEL: But how do we know?

KAREN: Because there's only two factors. All the factors of 1, and that's 1 and that has to work, and then itself, and that always has to work. The other thing I had to say was about 0. What about 0?

It is interesting to me that prime numbers, odd numbers, and 0 often pop up in discussions as the numbers that would be potential exceptions to the rules. We have on-going conversations about the factors of 0. Is there only one factor, or are there infinitely many? For now, we will leave it aside.

ALLAN: I think we should stick with whole numbers because a really high number might be harder to show it. We should use a middle number, like between one and a hundred.

TEACHER: So how many numbers would we have to try?

AURORA: Ten.

WEE-PING: All of them.

TEACHER: Do you remember when we looked at the switch-around rule? We found ways to show how it would always work, no matter what the numbers were. We used arrays and layers and turns to show people that no matter what number you used, it had to work. Those models were convincing to us, and we didn't have to use every number. Is there any way we could come up with something like that for this rule? Let's think about that for a few days. We'll come back to it then.

This is as far as we have come so far, but I hope to return to the idea soon. I am particularly intrigued by the method used by Susan and Marina when they showed the factors of 16 while simultaneously showing the factors of 48. As I think about it for myself, their model has a lot of potential. Couldn't you always start by breaking the original number into one of its factors? Then when the factors of one of those groups are found, those factors would *have* to be factors of the original number. Right? Put another way: If I take any number of things (m), and break that into equal groups, I'll get a factor (n) of that number. If I can break each of those groups into equal groups, I will get a factor of n. It follows that the factors of n would have to be factors of m because I would have several groups of factored groups of n. I am curious to see what kinds of models my students will offer as justification for this rule. What will it take to move them beyond wanting to test every number or search for exceptions?

CASE 32

Factors of factors, part 2

Alice

GRADE 3, MARCH

My students have been thinking about the question, Are the factors of a factor of a number also factors of that number? At the end of the last discussion on this topic, I had asked my students to think about how they could show that this rule works, no matter what numbers they were using. I had also reminded them that they had been able to do this by using models when they were investigating the switch-around rule. Now I wanted to learn if they would be able to do the same for this situation. So I asked whether or not all the factors of the factors of 120 were also factors of 120. As I observed students, I overheard one pair, Allan and Ben, talking about a "short cut" for checking for factors of factors. It seemed as though they were building on the idea Marina and Susan had shown us in the previous session. When the class gathered for a whole-group discussion about what they had learned, I asked Allan and Ben to share their idea first.

TEACHER: When I saw what Ben and Allan did to show how the factors of the factors were also factors of 120, I wondered if this might help us see how we could show it could work for all numbers and all factors.

BEN: We had ours in "eight-sticks," the way we do now.

The array he had in front of him looked like this:

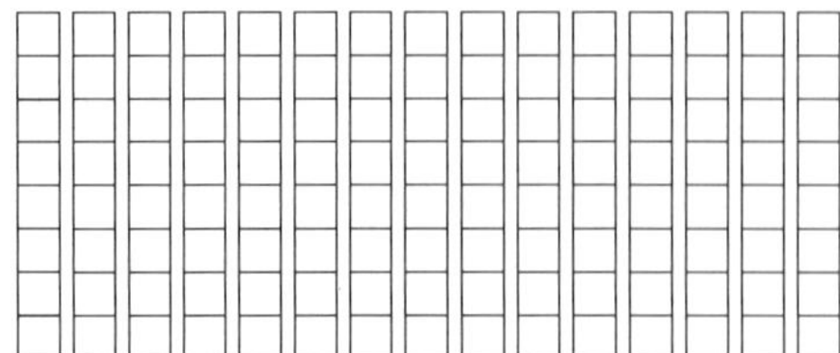

BEN: When you came over to us you asked a question if all the factors of 8 are also factors of 120. I said, "Sure!" and I just took one stick, and I just took the factors out.

GRADE 3, MARCH

TEACHER: Could you show us how you did that?

Ben broke one of the eight-sticks into two 4s, then four 2s, then eight 1s. I asked if someone could explain what it showed us about 8.

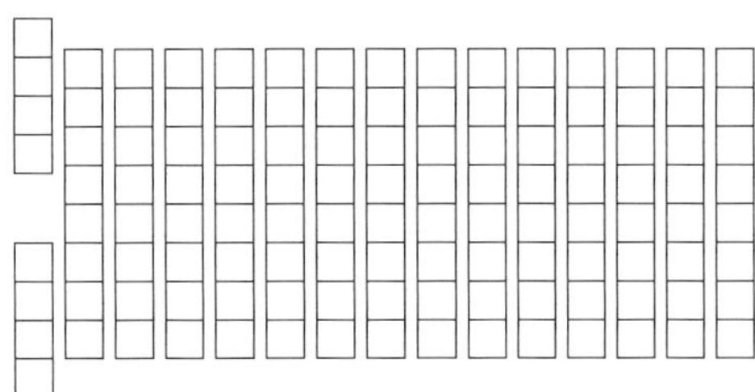

SUSAN: That you could keep splitting it in half.

STEVEN: It was showing us that just by breaking the stick in half, you can find all the factors of it.

TEACHER: So, Ben, did you find all the factors of 8?

BEN: Yes.

TEACHER: Allan, how did you two know that all those factors were also factors of 120?

ALLAN: Because all the multiples... Well, every stick is the exact same thing because it's made with the same number of cubes, so if there are certain factors of 8, they have to be the same factors of all the other 8s.

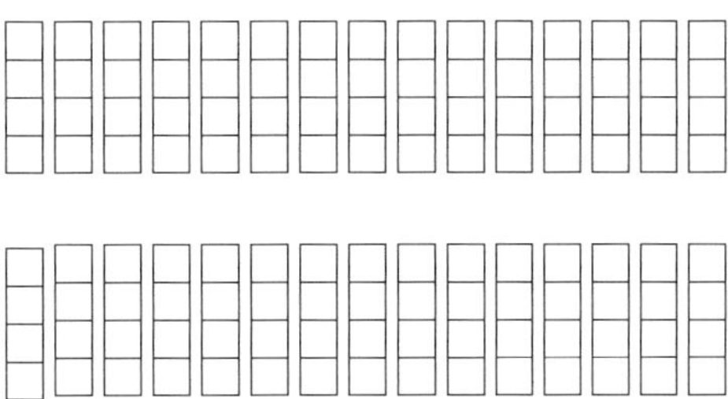

At this point, many students sighed with "Oh!" as a sign of acknowledgement that this idea could work for them, too.

TEACHER: Let's let that idea sit with us all for a few seconds, and then we'll see if anyone else can find a way of saying that idea in another way.

After a short, silent "think time," I asked Allan to call on someone who wanted to restate his idea. He picked Sharon.

SHARON: What they were saying, I think, is that since you could split *one* of the 8s into 1s or 2s or 4s, you could split *all* of the 8s into 1s or 2s or 4s, and that would mean that the 120, you can split into 1s or 2s or 4s.

Allan agreed that Sharon's paraphrase matched what he was saying.

KAREN: I think you can do that with every single number, unless, like... it's a prime number.

This prompted many murmurs from the group.

MARY: But 1 carries all its factors, and then there's the number itself, so it works for prime numbers, too.

KAREN: Oh, yeah, you can still do it with every number. I revised.

BEN: I think he (referring to Allan) means if all of them, no matter what number, if all of them are the same number, and you take one [stick] and find all its factors, it works for all of them.

Ben and Karen were moving the discussion into more generalized statements. I wonder what these students understood that allowed them to see this possibility in the model offered by Ben and his partner Allan. How many of the other students, who looked as though they understood the generalizations put forth by Ben and Karen, really did find it useful as a way of making a general argument or proof? What kind of evidence could I use to find out?

TEACHER: I want to ask you to think about something before we leave this for today. Do you think that what Ben and Allan offered to us is something we could use as a general argument for this idea about factors of factors? Does it work for us as a model, the way we had models for our switch-around rule for multiplication? Is this going to convince us that this idea about factors of factors works for all numbers?

Many students nodded, and many looked satisfied as a result of this shared experience. Ben and Allan's model did offer a compelling application to all numbers. Nonetheless, as we left for vacation that Friday afternoon, I was worried that the upcoming vacation break would cause us to lose some of the momentum we had gained over the past few days. I had seen many students begin to move toward generalizing this rule, and I wondered when they would have a chance to revisit these ideas. What is the next experience they will have that will cause them to reconsider this rule, and how will that experience move them to see the generalization? How can I keep the idea alive in the math work we have planned for when we return?

CASE 33

Factors of hundreds numbers

Jean

GRADE 4, JANUARY

For two days, my students worked on finding all of the factors of various hundreds numbers (multiples of 100). Some worked alone, some in pairs, and there were two small groups of students working on the activity. Although they were all doing the same assignment, strategies and approaches differed widely. Some students picked a number and skip-counted on a calculator to see if they landed on their hundreds number. Some students divided their hundreds number by the factor they were testing to see if the answer was a whole number. Some added with paper and pencil. Some tested factors in their heads. Some picked numbers at random to try. Some tried every number in order. Some could predict fairly accurately which numbers would be factors and tried those.

On the second day, we posted the number of factors that had been found for each hundreds number. We did not identify what the factors were, just how many had been found. Students developed ways to determine if they had all the factors. They would check their lists with each other, challenging each other's listings and double-checking their own.

We began the third day by assembling an organized chart on the board from their investigations. Under each hundreds number, 100 to 400, we listed its factors.

Jean

GRADE 4, JANUARY

Then I asked the following focus questions: What patterns do you see in looking at the factors of different hundreds numbers? How might the patterns help you in figuring out the factors of a hundreds number that is not yet on our chart?

Students were ready to offer a variety of observations:

SUE: All of the hundreds numbers have 1 as a factor, and they have, most of them have 2, and some, all of them have 10.

CHANG: All the second-to-last numbers in the columns go up by 50. For 100 the second-to-last factor is 50. For 200, it's 100. For 300, it's 150. For 400, it's 200.

SHAVON: Every one has its own number.

NANCY: All the numbers in the hundreds column, if you plus that number two times, you'll get something in the 200s column. Like 1, if you do it two times you'll get 2. There's a 2 in the second column. If you do 2 + 2 you get 4. If you do 4 + 4 you get 8. All the numbers in the 100 column, if you double them they're in the 200 column.

By the end of the class period, students had come up with 25 observations, which I wrote on a single sheet of paper. The following day, I handed out copies of the observations and asked students to select a few of the observations, determine if those observations are always true or sometimes true, and offer a proof.

Always True or Sometimes True?

1. 1, 2, 4, 5, 10, 20, 25, 50, and 100 are factors of all other hundreds numbers.
2. The next to the highest factors go up by 50.
3. The highest factor of a hundreds number is itself.
4. If you double the numbers in the 100 column, you get numbers in the 200 column.
5. Every two- or three-digit factor of hundreds numbers ends in 0 or 5, except 12 and 16.
6. There are a lot of 5s in the factors of hundreds numbers (5, 25, 50).
7. The factors of a hundreds number are in its double.

8. Factors of 100 and 500 follow a pattern: odd, even, even, odd, even, even.
9. If you take the 0s off a hundreds number, you get one of its factors.
10. 300 is the only hundreds number with 3 as a factor.
11. If you double a factor of a hundreds number, you get another factor of that number.
12. Each hundreds number has all the factors of 100.
13. The first two digits of a hundreds number are a factor of the number. 100 has 10 as a factor; 200 has 20 as a factor.
14. All other hundreds numbers will have more factors than 100.
15. Hundreds numbers have a lot more even factors than odd factors.
16. 7 is not a factor of a hundreds number.
17. The highest factor of a hundreds number is that number.
18. Many factors are multiples of 10.
19. The smallest factor times the largest factor is equal to the hundreds number.
20. The next to the smallest factor times the next to the largest factor is equal to the hundreds number.
21. 300 has factors that the other hundreds numbers do not have (3, 6, 12, 15, 30, 60, 75, 150, 300).
22. The factors of a factor of a hundreds number will also be factors of the hundreds number.
23. The number of factors of a hundreds number increases or decreases by multiples of 6 as you work with each larger hundred.
24. Every number has 1 and itself as factors.
25. 300 has the most factors.

In the opening discussion, I talked to the class about what constitutes a proof. Is it enough to test out some numbers? How many numbers do you have to test in order to claim that something is always true? What else can you do to say that something is always true?

Jean

GRADE 4, JANUARY

As the students began working, they selected observations at various levels of generality. Their proofs relied on their representations of multiplication or division, highlighting different interpretations of what these operations do.

The first observation on the list was, "1, 2, 4, 5, 10, 20, 25, 50 and 100 are always or sometimes factors of all the other hundreds numbers." Some children chose to prove the claim for each factor separately. For example, Betsy suggested, "All hundreds numbers are even and all even numbers can be divided by 2, so 2 is a factor of all hundreds numbers."

Shavon used the hundreds chart to show that 5 must be a factor of all hundreds numbers. First, she pointed to the 5s column and then, pointing to the 10s column, said that those numbers are multiples of 5. Because the hundreds numbers all appear in the 10s column, the hundreds numbers must have 5 as a factor.

When considering 25 as a factor, Shavon said that she thought of dollars and quarters. I asked the class to consider this idea. How many quarters are there in $2? $3? $4? $5?

TEACHER: So, what does that tell you about 25?

JOEY: That 25 goes into 100 four times, and so, however many dollars, there are, umm, there will be 4 quarters for each one—or four 25s.

TEACHER: So, what does that prove?

JOEY: That there's 25 in any hundred.

Still other children, also working from the first observation, interpreted it as "All factors of 100 are factors of other hundreds numbers." Thus, they offered a single proof for all 9 factors.

Chang, Ivan, and Khalid, working as a small group, thought about this claim in terms of skip-counting. Although they spoke in terms of specific numbers, they explained that they were talking about *all* factors of 100. Khalid used 25 as his first example. The number of 25s increases by 4 for each additional hundred.

Chang interrupted, excited by his own insights:

> Because 100 has those numbers as factors. Say I'm skipping by 2. I need, umm, 50 skips to get to 100. Umm. Just add 50 more, then you got a factor of 200. Just keep adding by 50s, you get to higher numbers, the other hundred numbers.

Jean

GRADE 4, JANUARY

When asked if there are any hundred numbers that you can't get to that way, Ivan spoke up. "700 has 7 hundreds in it. So, all those numbers are factors. You just have to take more jumps."

Virginia also wrote in terms of skip-counting to prove that the highest factor of a hundreds number is itself. "Yes, because you only have to make one jump."

Jon, Williamson, and James worked on observation #4, "If you double the numbers in the 100 column you get numbers in the 200 column." First, they wrote:

> I think this works because 100 is half of 200, and therefore, the factors of 100 are half of the factors of 200.

When I suggested that they might explore this generalization using arrays, the boys excitedly got back to work. First, they drew the following picture:

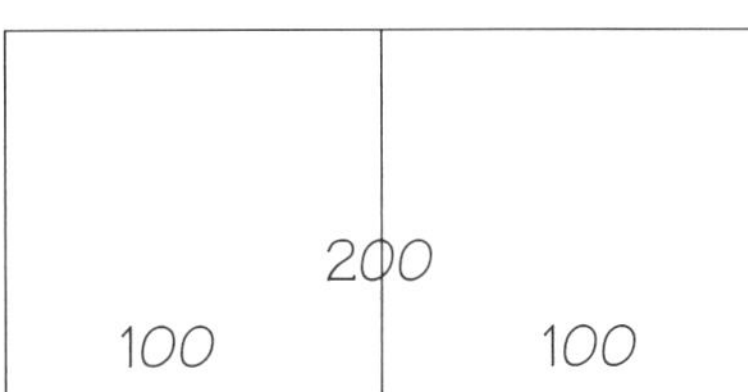

When asked if there was any way to see factors in the picture, Jon filled in some more numbers. "See, 20 × 10. And, inside here there is 10 × 10."

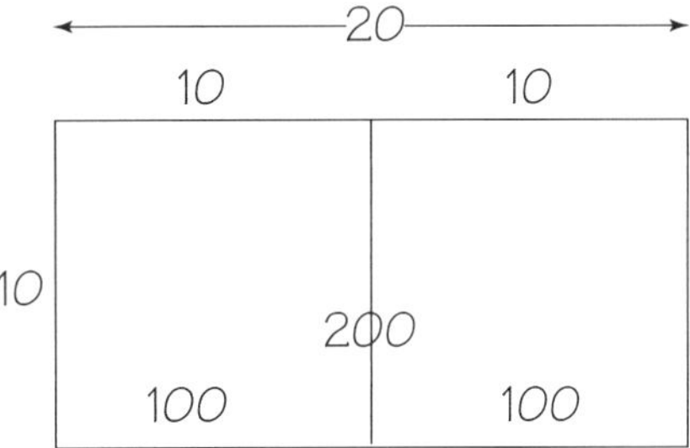

Jon's picture illustrates a rectangle with an area of 200. The measure of the vertical sides is 10, and the measure of the horizontal sides is 20. Half the rectangle, with an area of 100, has vertical sides of the same length (10) and horizontal sides half the length (10). However, Jon did not stop to explain this. Instead, he went ahead and drew a picture to demonstrate the same notion with another pair of factors. Starting with 50 × 4 as factors of 200, he cut his rectangle in half to show that half of 50, 25, is the corresponding factor of 100.

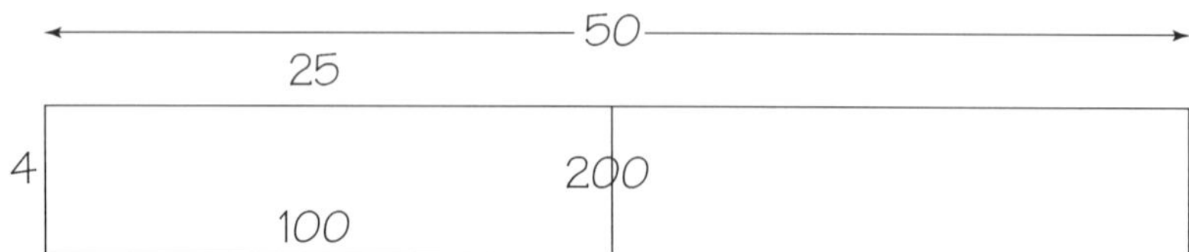

In fact, the original statement—if you double the factors of 100, you get factors of 200—is true. However, the boys shifted the claim to: if you halve the factors of 200, you get the factors of 100. This claim is problematic. For example, 25 is a factor of 200; but 12.5 is not a factor of 100. The boys did not consider any odd factors of 200.

Tyrone, who wrote about observation #25, "300 has the most factors," ended up working at a higher level of generality.

I don't think 300 has the most factors. Here's my proof. Because 600 is a multiple of 300, it has all the factors of 300 plus itself and 8.

I asked Tyrone about the claim that 600 has all the factors of 300. Here is Tyrone's written response:

> The reason for this is that any factor of a lower number will be a factor of any given multiple of that number. This is because you simply multiply the number the factor is being multiplied by as many times as the lower number goes into the multiple.

Thinking about this later, I saw Tyrone was able to keep track of which number is "the lower number," which is "the multiple," which is "the factor," and which is "the number the factor is being multiplied by." Indeed, Tyrone's explanation provides a good example of the power of algebraic notation in which the different quantities might be represented by a, b, c, n, and m. Although Tyrone wrote out his ideas in English, we can represent his claim as:

> If a is a factor of b, and c is a multiple of b, then a is a factor of c.
>
> This is because if $m \times a = b$ and $n \times b = c$, then $(n \times m) \times a = c$.

With just a few additional steps, Tyrone would have a formal proof.

> If a is a factor of b, then there is an integer, m, such that $m \times a = b$, and if c is a multiple of b, then there is an integer n, such that $n \times b = c$.
>
> By the Associative Law, $(n \times m) \times a = n \times (m \times a)$.

Since $b = m \times a$, $(n \times m) \times a = n \times (m \times a) = n \times b = c$.

Since $(n \times m)$ is an integer that, when multiplied by a, equals c, then a is a factor of c.

CASE 34

Products of factors

Rosalie

GRADES 5 AND 6, APRIL

I visited my colleague, Shelly Morrison, who teaches a fifth-sixth combination class. The lesson I observed was intriguing. Here's what happened:

Shelly began the lesson by referring to a problem from the textbook:

> Brian said, "If 6 is a factor of a number, then 2 and 3 are also factors of the number." Do you think Brian is right? Why or why not?

When she opened the floor for discussion, several students asserted that Brian was correct and offered examples of numbers that work. After a few minutes, Shelley summarized the observations.

TEACHER: We have 4 numbers for which this works: 36, 18, 24, and 12. Why?

CHLOE: Another thing is that 6 is an even number. Any time you have 6, 2 will go into the number.

DAN: Well, 3 is half of 6, so if 6 works so will 3.

GERI: As long as it is a factor of 6, it is a factor of 3.

In the moment the teacher chose not to correct Geri, who used the term *factor* when she meant *multiple*. It seemed that the flow of ideas was moving very quickly, so quickly that I couldn't capture it all in my notes. I did notice that at the end of the period, she checked in with Geri to make sure she understood the two words.

But as I said, in the moment, the discussion was lively with students offering ideas and changing their minds. Periodically, the whole-group discussion spontaneously broke into smaller conversations. In the midst of the flow of ideas, one student, Anthony, offered an observation.

Anthony: They might be saying 2 × 3 is 6 and 6 goes into 6. Then you need to try it with another number. Like 8. 2 × 4 is 8.

The teacher and students seemed to feel that Anthony's statement was beside the point, and no one responded to his idea.

As the discussion continued around ideas of 2, 3, 6, factors, and multiples, Anthony periodically said something about 2, 4, and 8, but he was ignored. After all, the class was working to figure something out about 2, 3, and 6.

The discussion wound around several ideas, and at one point, the teacher suggested the following strategy to refocus the discussion:

> Reread the original problem, which we'll call Statement 1:
>
> If 6 is a factor of a number, then 2 and 3 are also factors of the number.
>
> Then reread our most recent statement, which we'll call Statement 2:
>
> If 2 and 3 are factors of a number, then 6 is also a factor of the number.
>
> Think about how the two statements are related. I'll give people some quiet time to read and think.

The two statements are converses of one another, but that subtlety was not apparent to most students, though Anthony, who was taking a broader perspective, could see a difference. After 4 or 5 quiet minutes, he spoke up.

Anthony: I think I found a fault with Statement 2. 2 and 4 are factors of 12, and 2 × 4 = 8; 8 can't go into 12.

In response to his classmates' protest, Anthony continued: "I'm just saying you can't do this with all numbers. You can do it with odd numbers."

Suddenly, Anthony's concerns began to make sense to his classmates and teacher. He was trying to determine the general principle behind the specific example of 2, 3, and 6.

ANTHONY: I'm talking about a whole different number; 2 and 4 are factors of 8; 2 and 4 are factors of 12; but 8 can't go into 12.... I'm trying to see if it works on all numbers. If it is a rule, it needs to work on all numbers.

TEACHER: I see his point. What if we change the numbers 2, 3, and 6 to any two numbers and their product? For what kinds of numbers will Statement 1 hold? For what kinds of numbers will Statement 2 hold?

With help from the teacher in clarifying and articulating his point, the class began to take on Anthony's question as their own, particularly focusing on Statement 2. Students were pretty convinced that the statement, "If 2 and 3 are factors of a number, then so is 6," is true. However, the statement, "If 2 and 4 are factors of a number, then so is 8," is not. Now the question became, under what conditions is the claim true that if two numbers are factors of a third, then so is their product? Anthony had suggested, "You can do it with odd numbers." Now, his classmates offered other conjectures:

NEIL: I think you have to have two primes for this to work. This was 2 and 3. It doesn't work with 2 and 4.

TEACHER: So, you are saying these are prime, and that is why it works?

SALLY: Maybe if the two numbers can't go into each other. That might be right.

The class continued in this vein and, by the end of the lesson, generated a series of hypotheses about the number pairs: They both have to be odd; they both have to be prime; one number can't go into the other number; one number must be even and the other odd; one number must be even and the other prime. They are still working on this idea.

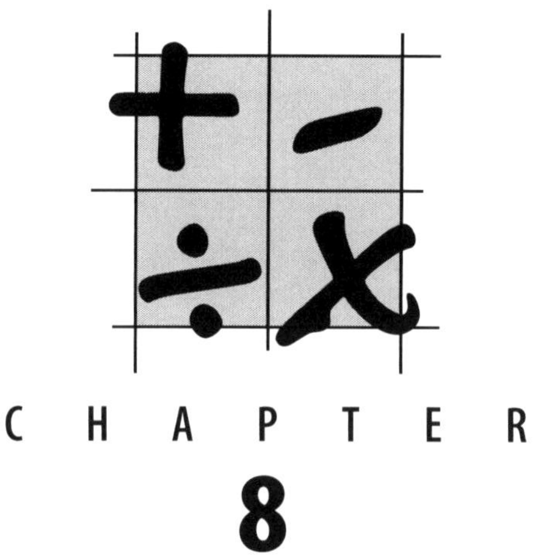

CHAPTER

8

The World of Arithmetic From Different Points of View

Stephen Monk, Department of Mathematics, University of Washington

1 • Introduction

In Case 1 of this book, Dolores, the teacher–author, and her third-grade students have a series of conversations about the possibilities for adding even numbers that total the "number of the day" (the number of days they have been in school). After several conversations, some students' responses are no longer based on specific computations; they notice patterns in their calculations and answers that convince them of the generalization: The sum of even numbers is *always* even. On the thirty-third day, when the teacher asks if it is possible to add even numbers to make 33, one student says: "YOU CAN'T DO IT!!! Even 10 + 10 + 10 + 2 + 2 can't do it. Sorry, you can't do it." Another student writes, "Even numbers plus even numbers always add up to even, and 33 is odd." Yet, some students continue to take a computational approach, assuming that it is possible to find such numbers and that it is just a matter of getting the correct combination. As Dolores says, "I think it is still a 'number specific' idea for about half of the children. I expect they will jump into trying many combinations of even numbers to make the number 39 and 41 and maybe even 55. It may take time for them to get it."

How is it that some students notice patterns, make generalizations, and even begin to give reasons for them, while others stay in "number specific" mode, adding one combination after another, hoping to come upon the correct answer? How do students develop a way of thinking that leads to generalizations? How can they be encouraged to engage in problems that will enable them to make generalizations? Do certain kinds of tasks elicit such thinking more than others? Are certain forms of classroom community more supportive of it than others? As Dolores asks, "Can they [students] help each other make generalizations?" Implicit in her writing is the difficult question of how a teacher can promote this kind of thinking in the classroom.

As one reads the cases in this book, the richness and value of thinking more generally, of seeing patterns, making generalizations, and giving explanations for them become very evident, as does the challenge of helping students become more adept at this process. Many mathematics educators observe that this kind of thinking underlies school algebra, an idea they emphasize by calling it "algebraic thinking" or "algebraic reasoning." They argue that if students were more adept at algebraic reasoning, they would be more successful at algebra when they study it later in their schooling. However, in order for teachers of grades K–8 to commit valuable resources of time and energy to such a goal, it is necessary to make the case for it in terms of the ongoing mathematical lives of the students in these grades and not in terms of how it will better their mathematical lives in the distant future. Does this goal conflict with the objective of helping students achieve computational fluency? Or do the goals support one another in some way? If algebraic reasoning does not bring rewards in terms of mathematical power in grades K–8, then activities devoted to it cannot be sustained in the long run.

This essay is intended to help teachers and mathematics educators who have used this book explore how generalizing about numbers and operations can support students' mathematical work in the elementary and middle grades. To do this, it is first necessary to examine what we mean by phrases such as "making generalizations" and "justifying generalizations" as we apply them to everyday life. We must also consider what particular meanings these phrases take on as they are used in connection with mathematics. We should ask ourselves:

- What are the ground rules and expectations in mathematics for establishing that a particular statement is true?
- Are there basic capacities or skills that support a student's ability to make and justify generalizations?
- What particular challenges will arise in classrooms in which students are making and supporting mathematical generalizations?

2 • Generalization and Justification in Mathematics

Generalizing is a natural human tendency, but methods of justifying generalizations vary from context to context. Mathematical justification is based on logic.

According to the dictionary[1], a generalization is a "statement, law, principle, or proposition that relates to every member of a class, kind, or group." As such, people make generalizations quite often. Generalizing is a basic aspect of human thinking and is critical to the way we make our way in the world. This is true of children as well as adults. A toddler quickly notices that getting too far out of her parents' sight brings a quick and strong response. Based on her observations, she has made a generalization relating her movement and her parents' behavior. Much of a child's language development depends on the formation and careful refinement of categories and the assignment of names to them. These large furry creatures are "cats." Oh, but the ones that bark are "dogs." Cats are the ones that say "meow."

---

[1] *Merriam-Webster Online Dictionary*. 2004. http://www.merriam-webster.com

As adults, we carry around in our heads an incredible array of generalizations: "They serve hot dogs for school lunch on Wednesday," "Fish sleep with their eyes open," "The sum of two even numbers is an even number." From a mathematical point of view, there is an important distinction to be made as to the basis of one's belief that a particular generalization is true—one's justification for it. One might carefully observe the pattern of the menus in the school lunch and eventually conclude that "they serve hot dogs for school lunch on Wednesday." In this case, *observation* alone is sufficient as a form of justification. However, because few of us have ever seen fish sleep, we cannot rely on observation in order to justify generalizations about whether their eyes are open or shut when they do so. In this case, we must rely on *authority*, usually in the form of the findings of experts. Neither observation nor authority is generally acceptable in mathematics as a means of justifying generalizations. When Dolores's students consider the statement, "The sum of two even numbers is an even number," almost all understand that they must support this generalization without appealing to authority. Many feel that the only alternative is through direct observation, to try out all possible combinations of even numbers and observe whether the answer in each case is even or not. But other students recognize that this is impossible because there are infinitely many combinations to check. Dealing with this difficulty is one of the great challenges students face as they learn to justify their generalizations.

It is central to mathematics, as a discipline, that justification is always based on *logic*. If I want to convince other people of the truth of a generalization I have made, I can only do so by citing other statements that they and I agree on and by then establishing, in strict logical steps, that anyone who agrees with these statements must also believe my new generalization. For instance, if others and I agree that an even number is a number that can be written as another whole number plus itself (for instance, that 14 is even because it is 7 + 7), then in order to justify a new generalization about even numbers, I must proceed by a chain of strictly logical deductions, from our agreed-upon definition of what an even number is to my new generalization. However, if others do not agree with my definition of an even number, then I have no way to convince them of the truth of my generalization unless we can find a definition that we do agree on (for instance, that an even number is one that is arrived at by counting by 2s, starting at 0). At this point, I am able to move by strictly logical steps from this definition to my generalization.

One can say, then, that in mathematics we do not use logic to establish *truths* in any absolute sense, but that we use logic to establish *chains of deduction* from agreed-upon statements, definitions, and understandings to other statements that follow by logical deduction. However, every chain must have its initial link. A group of people cannot agree on the truth of a mathematical statement unless they have made some initial agreements and assumptions. Once they have done this, they can use logic to establish other statements that can be included in their catalog of true statements. The statements in this catalog can then serve as the basis for establishing new true statements, and so forth. It all depends on those initial agreements. When a group of people say that a given mathematical statement is "true" or "proved" or "valid," what they really mean is that the given statement can be logically proven from other statements they already agree are true.

The commitment to justification by logic is one of the most important features of mathematics. One might say that it is a defining property of the subject. When mathematicians communicate about a mathematical statement (or generalization) they have made, they are likely to sketch a proof that the statement is true, as if the only issue is the logical validity of the statement. In fact, a proof serves a number of different communicative functions among mathematicians, all at the same time. It is supposed to help the listener make sense of the statement, to explain why it is true, and to generally persuade and *teach* the listener about the ideas contained in the statement. In this book, these functions are also being carried out by students' arguments in support of their assertions. They are teaching, explaining, helping others to make sense, and establishing logical validity.

3 • The *All* problem

Once students realize that it is impossible to test all numbers, they are faced with the question of whether it is possible to make claims about ALL and, if so, how to justify those claims.

The study of properties of numbers such as even/odd, factors, and prime numbers is part of a branch of mathematics, called "number theory," that dates back to the ancient Greeks. Along with the study of plane geometry, number theory was in full flower by 500 BC, nearly two thousand years before our base-10 number system. Number theory has always been a favorite subject for amateur mathematicians because one can quickly arrive at intriguing questions about numbers and their relationships without years of training.

Making conjectures about patterns in the properties of numbers is only the beginning of number theory. As soon as one has found a pattern, one immediately wants to try it out on other numbers. If it still works, several questions quickly arise: Why is this true? How does it work? Will it *always* be true? Will this be true for *all* numbers of this type? Addressing these questions can lead to new questions that are surprisingly deep.

For example, in Case 33, the students in Jean's fourth-grade class have been making observations and conjectures about the factors of "hundreds numbers" (numbers that are multiples of 100). When Jean asks them "What patterns do you see in looking at the factors of different hundreds numbers?" the class creates twenty-five different statements. Many of these statements are very general and cover more than the specific numbers they have been dealing with. When students note that "each hundreds number has all the factors of 100," they are grounded in the arithmetic of particular calculations they have carried out and are also thinking in general about how numbers fit together.

When we examine the twenty-five statements made in Jean's class, a crucial distinction among the general statements begins to emerge. This distinction plays an enormous role in many of the classroom cases in the Casebook and in the subject of mathematics itself. Jean's class begins by listing various hundreds numbers and, at first, many of their statements refer only to these specific numbers. Then in addition to asking for patterns in the numbers they have before them, Jean asks, "How might the patterns help you in figuring out the factors of a hundreds number that is not yet on our chart?" In other words, they are not only accountable for the truth of their statements about the list of numbers they already have but for *all* hundreds numbers. There are an endless—an infinite—number of such numbers. This is the beginning of what I call the *All* problem: How can we make and trust in statements about an infinite number of numbers? Isn't it strange to imagine that we can say something that is true about numbers we will never see, about more numbers than we can ever count? Can this really be done?

When Dolores, the third-grade teacher in Case 1, asks her students "How can we be sure an even number added to an even number will give us an answer that is even?" most feel that they can never be sure because doing so would require that they check an endless number of addition problems, which they know cannot be done. One of the students,

Zoe, simply states that "I know it will add to an even number because $4 + 4 = 8$ and $8 + 8 = 16$." She feels that she knows enough from these two examples to be confident in the truth of the generalization. It is quite possible that Zoe also has in mind other such particular examples to support her belief. However, the basis of belief, the justification, for Zoe is to check particular examples, perhaps some examples that seem very significant, and on the basis of the outcome, make a prediction: "Based on what I have seen thus far, it looks like this pattern will persist." This approach is very common in grades K–8 and does not disappear altogether, even among college students who do not take on the skeptical stance that characterizes mathematical justification.

We see a different reaction to the *All* problem in Lucy's third-grade class in Case 4. In response to the same question that Dolores's class is discussing, Amanda states that "two evens, no matter what they are, have to equal an even." She gives a proof of this statement in terms of counting by 2s, which she demonstrates with the help of cubes. "I have this, both of them (the two sticks) count by 2s, so if I put them on top of each other, you keep counting by 2s, and then you get to an even number." Another student, Elizabeth, works very hard to absorb what Amanda has said. It might seem that Elizabeth is having difficulty with the particulars of Amanda's statements, but she then says: "Well, I don't know, because in some cases, well, um, I can't really think of it now, but like, if you have one that was an even plus an even, if like, I haven't figured this out, but sometimes maybe it could equal an odd."

After responses by both Amanda and Lucy, the teacher, Elizabeth says: "So she's saying she already knows that it always equals it." Lucy goes on to say: "Elizabeth seemed quite close to understanding Amanda's argument, but she just doesn't seem able to make a claim about *all* even numbers." This is not surprising, however, because a claim about *all* numbers is quite a claim. Lucy also recognizes that this is not a sign of weakness on Elizabeth's part. To recognize that "it's not sufficient to argue that a generalization is always true simply by looking at particular examples" is "key toward understanding the need for mathematical proof based on *logic* rather than example." This is an important step. To make an argument strong enough to cover an infinite number of numbers will demand new and very different ways of thinking. In order to meet this challenge, a student must first acknowledge that there is a genuinely deep problem to be solved.

Although it does not quite convince Elizabeth, Amanda's justification in Case 4 for her proposition that "two evens, no matter what they are, have to equal an even" has an important feature, the use of representations. The cubes Amanda has arranged play a critical role in her response to the *All* problem. The criterion that Amanda is using for a number to be even is that you land on it when counting by 2s. If we have two even numbers, both represented by sticks of cubes, then we add them by joining the sticks of cubes, as in the diagram below showing addition of 6 and 4.

As Amanda says: "If I put them on top of each other, you keep counting by 2s, and then you get to an even number."

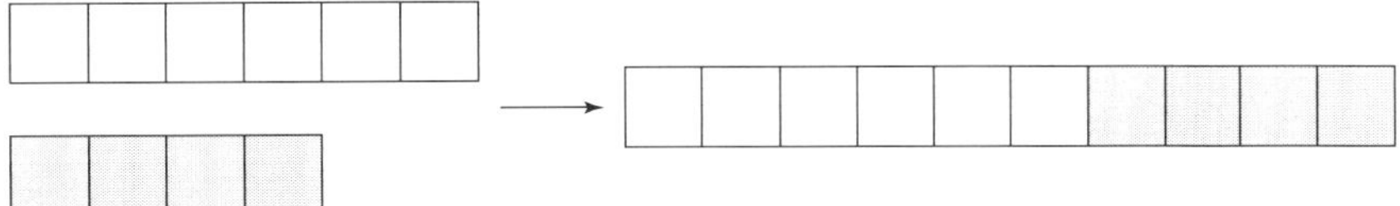

But there is something subtle going on here that is of great significance, and that we must explore further. It comes up throughout the Casebook and throughout mathematics. Amanda is making a general claim about what happens when you add *any* two even numbers. However, her argument involves a particular stick of 6 cubes and another stick of 4 cubes. Can one say that this is a valid argument for a generalization when it is based on particular numbers? In fact, this kind of use of "representative examples" is a common practice in mathematics, one that is used to address the *All* problem, both in teaching and in informal conversations among mathematicians. There is some evidence for saying that, in the way she has used the sticks of cubes, Amanda wants us to be thinking about *any* pair of even numbers, even though her sticks have 6 and 4 cubes, respectively. The same argument would work if the two sticks had 8 and 14 cubes, or any other two numbers as long as you land at the end of each stick when counting by 2s (i.e., any two even numbers). Amanda does not make this point explicitly, but I think it is there, implicitly, in the way she uses and talks about the cubes.

An extension of Amanda's approach would be to make a diagram that shows two even numbers of blocks but without indicating specific numbers. I have sketched such a diagram on the next page, using the idea that the blocks with the letter *e* in them are where one lands when counting by 2s. The diagram shows that when the two sticks are combined, the alternating sequence of *not-e* and *e* continues so that an *e* falls on the last cube. This diagram increases complexity, perhaps without any increase in persuasiveness from Amanda's original cube model.

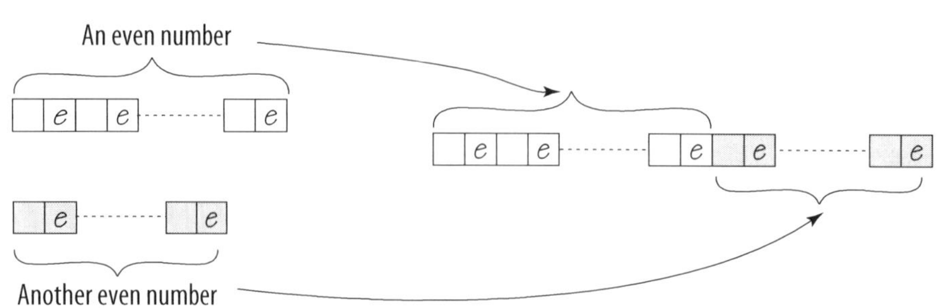

When we review the cases discussed in this book, it is not difficult to see how the students in these classes can benefit from such explorations and conversations. They are learning to articulate their thinking, justify their conclusions, use diagrams to communicate, and see new relationships among numbers. In addition, they are encountering unfamiliar mathematical concepts such as *factor* and *divisibility*, notions that will be useful throughout their study of mathematics. But there is another aspect to their experience here that we see throughout the Casebook. By engaging with these questions about concepts like even/odd and factors, they have shifted their focus and are seeing arithmetic in a new way. The experience of arithmetic has generally been, for most students, one of *actions taken*, of combining numbers, of counting and carrying, of multiplying and manipulating numbers, to get new numbers. By contrast, the conversations discussed in these cases are about *relationships* among numbers, of when they hold and when they do not hold, of when they are maintained under the operations of addition and multiplication. This new focus should not supplant the more ordinary one. A thorough understanding of K–8 mathematics depends on being able to pursue both fluency with computation *and* reasoning about the operations, moving back and forth between these perspectives.

4 • Making things explicit

A key reason for making generalizations explicit is to make them available to use as a tool for solving problems.

Many of the generalizations we use in ordinary life remain implicit, even as they guide our behavior. For example, the rules that govern sentence structure and grammar in English can be seen as generalizations about parts of speech. Students learn to correctly form the past tense of verbs, "I paint," "I painted"; "I laugh," "I laughed." They also learn that there are "irregular verbs" so that we say "I go" but not "I goed." They do this without making these generalizations explicit. Similarly, we all know many social rules and are guided by generalizations without making them explicit. No one ever explains that the waiter in a restaurant will not usually sit down at the table to have an extended conversation. Few of us have ever explicitly stated this generalization. It is "just something you know." However, in mathematics, *making a generalization means making it explicit*. There are many reasons for this. Among them are that one cannot justify a statement that has not been made explicit. Another reason is that, if justification is a matter of building up chains of deduction, then any group of people whose goal it is to have an agreed-upon set of generalizations must keep an active and explicit catalog of these generalizations. Yet another reason is that, when a generalization is made explicit, it becomes available for us as a strategy for solving problems in a variety of situations.

For example, consider Case 8 in Chapter 2, "Finding Relationships in Addition and Subtraction." Kate's second graders, asked to find equations with sums of 100, respond with a series of number sentences, $99 + 1 = 100$; $98 + 2 = 100$; $97 + 3 = 100$; and so forth. Scott explains, "We're taking away from that number and adding to the other number." Kate then asks Scott to demonstrate what he is thinking with some cubes. He shows a stack of ten cubes, which is then progressively transformed into one stack of 9 cubes and another stack of 1 cube, then one stack of 8 cubes and another stack of 2 cubes, and then one stack of 7 cubes and another stack of 3 cubes, and so forth. Using Scott's representation with cubes, other students are able to articulate further the general principle underlying this situation, that they are "taking 1 from one pile and adding that 1 to the other pile.... The amount stays the same, but you keep adding more to the other side." While Kate is "delighted" with her students' understanding, her "real goal is to help them make this understanding useful." She wonders if they would be able to use what they have just learned in order to transform the addition problem $39 + 14$ into an easier problem.

Certainly, one of the goals in Kate's classroom involves finding answers to particular computations. That is, however, secondary to her goal of trying to help her students develop computational *strategies*, a form of generalization that involves a sense of what happens in a broad range of computational situations. In order for such strategies to be accessible for use in a variety of contexts, they must be based on sound general principles that are also made explicit. Thus, even though the activities in

Kate's class are oriented toward computation, they ultimately have a great deal in common with the activities in the cases about factors or about odds and evens—noticing patterns across classes of numbers and making them explicit.

Kate's question of her students, whether they are able to use what they learned from the sentences about numbers that add to 100 (or add to 10) in order to determine the sum 39 + 14, suggests a new goal for students: that they be able to *use* a generalization arrived at in one situation as a tool for solving a problem in a related situation. Historically, this has been a central goal in mathematics, to form generalizations that can be used as *portable tools* that can be carried around and applied in a variety of situations. This is a challenging and complex goal. Not only does it require that computational strategies be made explicit and that they be in a form that makes them usable in a variety of settings, but they must be understood by students in a way that makes them accessible in the future so that when the students are in a new situation, they will be able to recall these strategies and use them appropriately. We get a clearer sense of the complexities of these goals by studying some of the other cases in this chapter.

The kindergarten students in Case 6, written by Lola, are playing the game Double Compare, in which each of two students places two numbered cards on the table. The student whose cards add to the greater sum "wins." Lola notices that when two students put two cards out and there is one number in common between their two pairs (for example, one student has 6 and 3, and the other, 6 and 1), then, rather than add, they look at the cards that are different and conclude that the student with the card with the greater number wins. Later, when she asks them about this, "Martina said that 6 and 3 is more than 6 and 1 because the 3 is bigger than the 1." When Lola asks, "What about the 6s?" Martina replies, "They're the same." Paul adds, "They don't matter. You don't have to pay attention to the 6s." As Lola says, her students "were close to articulating" what they were seeing.

The difficulty of stepping back and making a generalization explicit when one is engrossed in a task raises the question of why it is important to do so. If one knows how to do things, isn't it sufficient to just do them? Why must one articulate what one is thinking about in words, pictures, or even a formula? One answer is that if a computational strategy is not articulated, then it is less likely to be used in other situations. Genuine computational fluency results from applying strategies that are well understood and made explicit, not simply from repeated application of rules.

The students in Monica's fourth-grade class in Case 9 are dealing with a different aspect of the challenge suggested by Kate's case, using a generalization arrived at in one situation as a tool for solving a problem in another situation. They have been working on a problem that involves weights of apples as they dehydrate. After arriving at the answer of 45 to the problem 145 – 100, they are working on the related problem, 145 – 98. The students believe that, because 98 is 2 less than 100, then the answer to this new problem is either 43 or 47. They should either add the 2 to 45 or subtract it from 45; they are not at all certain which. This reasoning in itself represents a level of generalization; these students have stepped outside of the particulars of the numbers involved and are looking for a more general principle to guide them to the answer. A student in "number specific" mode might not have even noticed the relationship between the two problems, 145 – 100 and 145 – 98.

Brian's response to the question of whether the answer is more or less than 45 is to say, "It's like you have this big thing to take away and then you have a little thing to take away. So you have more." He then illustrates this with a diagram saying "See, this is the apple at first. And you take some away and have some left. Then you take away 98 grams instead, so it's over here."

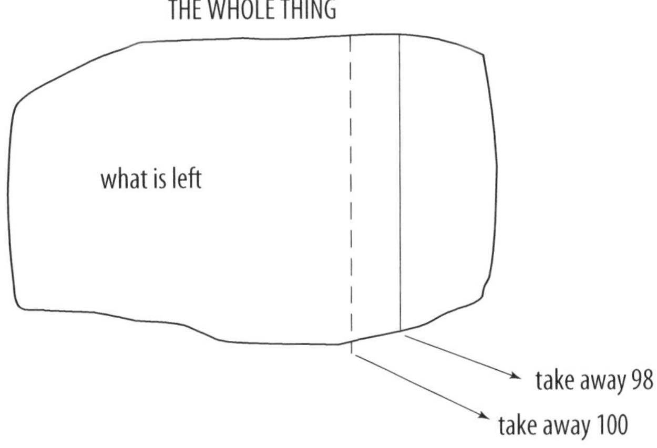

Rebecca then reiterates and amplifies this explanation. Instead of referring to an apple, however, she uses a "hunk of bread" to explain her thinking. Rebecca says, "...You can take a tiny bite or a bigger bite. If you take away smaller you end up with bigger."

One way to interpret what has taken place here is that Brian and Rebecca have arrived at a general principle that they have represented with a diagram and in words. It is in the language and imagery of fourth graders, but it represents a general principle. A mathematician might say, "If we have two quantities, A and B, and you know that A is less than B, and if both quantities are subtracted from a larger quantity C, then $C - A$ is larger than $C - B$." This idea can be compressed even further into symbols, but the symbolic notation expresses the same relationship that Brian and Rebecca describe. Although the work of these students is embedded in a particular situation, with its details of apples and weights, Brian and Rebecca have stepped outside the particular situation and articulated a generalization that links this situation to a general class of situations.

It is worth noting the role of the representation in this situation. There are several distinct parts to this problem: the starting weight, 145; the landmark, 100; the "next weight," 98; the first difference of 45; and the difference of 2 between 98 and 100. Although it is not clear how Brian arrived at his principle, which he first gave in words, the diagram plays an important role in helping others see what is going on and step away from the particular numbers. This diagram brings together all of the important parts of the problem and shows their relationships well enough for students to be able to reason about them and gain access to the generalization that helps solve the problem. The diagram and Brian's verbal explanation play an important role in making the generalization explicit and available for other students to consider.

5 • Working with models of operations

At the elementary level, a major approach to justifying generalizations involves models of the operations. When students at once hold both what they know about computing and the models the operations are built from, this "binocular (two-sighted) vision" allows them to reason about the operations.

In Case 12, "Does order matter when adding?," Kate, the teacher, begins by asking her second graders "if it would matter if we added 20 + 10 or we added 10 + 20." Her students respond with a "resounding no." When they continue this conversation the next day, Kate has her students imagine that they are talking to the principal: "Mr. Valen is standing here and he doesn't believe you, so you've got to be really careful to convince him." She uses this technique because she wants to help her students "get past the notion that 'we all know this, so what else is there to say?'" Kate is encouraged by the fact that, as her students work in pairs on this task, more of her students are able to move beyond the certainty of a simple unexamined answer than had been the case earlier. It seems evident that "not only does [order not matter] for any pair of numbers but students also have such a clear idea that the order doesn't matter, they know it will not matter regardless of how many numbers are involved."

When Kate asks Corey how he knows that he can combine four 10-rods and one 100-flat in any order to make the number 140, he says: "You're just switching them around and not adding any or taking any away.... You're just switching them around and putting them in different spots." By keeping the operation of addition closely associated with the model of combining sets, Corey and his classmates are confident of their claims. A set does not change as you look at subsets differently and move them around. Students can use this set to model many arithmetic sentences that *do* look different but are the same because they correspond to the same set. As Kate points out, this depends on the property of "conservation" of a set: "You can move the numbers around, you can break them up, and as long as you don't add any or take any away, it [the set] stays the same when you put them all back together." Her students' explanations rely on models of the operations on which their understanding was initially built, even when they no longer refer to those models in carrying out routine computation.

Lola's question in Case 11, "Does order matter when counting?" and Kate's question, "Does order matter when adding?" get at the foundation of arithmetic, the basic properties of the operations. In both of these cases, particular numbers and particular answers are relatively unimportant. The discussions among students in these cases approach an articulation of the Commutative Law of Addition.

In the cases in the book, the shift of students' attention that takes place, from numbers and answers to properties of operations and justification, brings to the surface a number of complexities of students' learning that are not evident in more conventional arithmetic lessons. Kate comments early in her case that "there has been a shift in the children's thinking.... Most of them are operating on a numerical level and there are far fewer children who need to count on in order to do computation. ...I wondered if... operating numerically reflects the potential to think more abstractly about these ideas." However, what we see in this case is that moving to a "numerical level" does not mean permanently moving away from thinking about sets of objects, illustrated by cubes in Kate's case. Rather, it means being able to operate with numbers *and* being able to move back to the sets that underlie our operations with numbers. This "binocular vision" is critical for elementary school students' reasoning about operations. It captures what they know about computation, and at the same time, the sets or models the operations are built from.

Case 13, "The 'switch-around' rule," reveals another issue in dealing with the foundations of arithmetic. After her students have considered several examples of number sentences that involve adding pairs of numbers in which the order does not matter (so that the numbers can be "switched around"), the third-grade teacher, Alice, writes on the board what she considers a summary of what they have said: "When you add two numbers together, you can change the order and still get the same answer." However, the next day, when she asks them to write the switch-around rule in their own words and to give examples, she is surprised that the responses are far more varied than she anticipated. Many statements and examples involve subtraction, whereas Alice was assuming that the conversation was exclusively about addition.

For those of us familiar with the landscape of the world of arithmetic, the four operations stand out as extremely prominent landmarks. We understand that a statement like "order does not matter," when made about one operation, does not tell us about other operations, even if they seem similar to the given operation. Statements of this kind are attributes of specific operations. This is true in the same sense that a statement like "Cats purr when they are content" is specific to one species of animal and not to other animals, regardless of whether they are very much like cats. Coming to understand that operations are very important features of the world of arithmetic and that they have distinctive characteristics is an important outcome of conversations like the one in Alice's class. Students do not come equipped with this understanding. Their attention has been on *numbers* and acting on numbers. For many students, the *operations* have yet to surface as separate entities that have distinct properties. They need to be engaged in the kinds of conversation we see in the second half of Case 13, in which students give reasons why they think switch-arounds "only work when it's a plus" and consider the complications that arise when they are subtracting. Sorting through these issues is an opportunity to further differentiate these operations from one another.

When students are pressed to logically justify that a certain property holds for addition of whole numbers, they appeal to a common understanding of whole-number addition, as joining sets of things. Two whole numbers are added by considering two distinct sets that have as many objects as the two given numbers and then bringing those two sets together. The sum of the two numbers is the number of objects in the combined set. By applying the same approach to subtraction, removing one set from another, students can explain why switching around numbers does not yield the same answer. Here again, students apply their binocular vision, referring to underlying models of familiar operations.

6 • Operations in relation to one another

To further explore the properties of an operation, one can examine its relationship to other operations, or one can contrast the operation with another operation.

The sixth graders in Azar's class (Case 20) are discussing how it is possible to have two different equations for the same situation. They are discussing the quantities, A, the actual weight of an object, and S, the weight of the same object as it appears on a scale that is slightly inaccurate. Some students connect these quantities using the equation, $A + 2 = S$, which says that 2 pounds should be added to the actual weight in order to get the scale weight. Other students connect these quantities with the equation $S - 2 = A$, which says that 2 pounds should be subtracted from the scale weight of an object in order to get its actual weight. The two equations represent the same underlying relationship between the quantities. This is what is meant by the statement that the operations of addition and subtraction are inversely related. The first graders in Nadine's class in Case 21 and Daisy's class in Case 22 are in the early stages of addressing the same idea in a more specific way using particular numbers. While the conversation among the first graders is different than among sixth graders, all are working toward the fact that addition and subtraction are inversely related. While this fact is very important in itself, much of its significance for students may be in their recognition that these operations are distinct mathematical entities with their own properties.

Alice's two cases in Chapter 5 (Cases 23 and 24), "Is one acting just like zero? part 1" and "Is one acting just like zero? part 2" are built from an assumption, shared by most of the students in Alice's third-grade class, that there are parallels between the two operations of addition and multiplication and that in these parallels, the special numbers, 0 and 1, play analogous roles. The discussion in this class results from a question that one student, Martha, raises and repeatedly comes back to, "Is one acting just like zero?" This question leads students to shift their attention back and forth between the operations of addition and multiplication and to test their knowledge of the meanings and models of these operations: How do we say in ordinary language what 60×1 means? How is this like $60 + 0$?

One of the lasting effects for Alice's students of considering these questions is that they are developing a much sharper awareness of addition and multiplication as operations, each with its own separate properties. There are important parallels between the two operations, but they are also different from one another.

The cases in Chapter 6, "Multiplying in Clumps," also raise issues about the connections and differences between two distinct operations and how these are maintained and justified by an underlying model, as well as by numerical and symbolic notation. The focus in this chapter is on the relationship between addition and multiplication known as the Distributive Law.

Students in Lucy's third-grade classroom in Case 26, "Bunches of flowers," are working on a problem in which there are 4 bunches of flowers picked in the morning and 3 bunches of flowers picked in the evening. Each bunch contains 8 flowers. Some students say that there are 7 bunches of flowers altogether with 8 flowers in each so that there are 56 flowers in all. Other students say that 32 flowers were picked in the morning and 24 flowers were picked in the evening so that, altogether, 56 flowers were picked. The challenge for these students is to see that there are two distinct methods being used here, to recognize that they both give the same answer, and to understand why this is so. That these two methods produce the same result is what the Distributive Law tells us.

In general, if we have one bunch of groups (B groups) and another bunch of groups (C groups), and each group has A things in it, then we can figure out how many things we have altogether using two different methods. The first is to multiply A times the total number of groups: $A \times (B + C)$. The second is to multiply each number of groups by A and then add the two products: $(A \times B) + (A \times C)$. The Distributive Law tells us that these two methods give the same answer. This generalization can be represented in terms of the diagram below. It can also be represented in symbolic notation as $A \times (B + C) = (A \times B) + (A \times C)$.

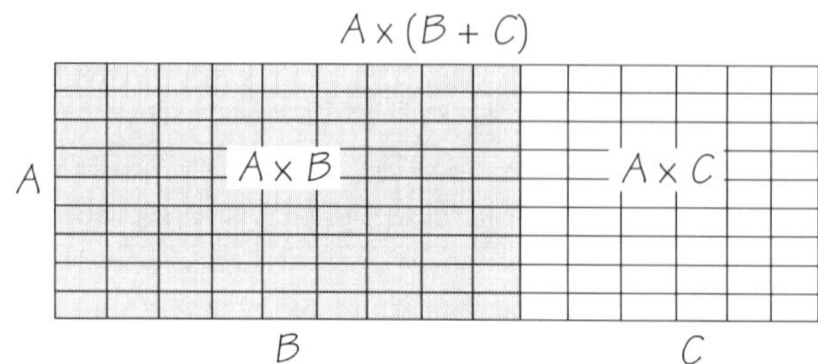

What the cases in Chapter 6 have in common is that students are working between two levels. The first level involves models of the operations and of sets of things, and the second level incorporates the use of numbers and symbols. The model helps them keep the various parts of the situation organized and is used to justify the connections they make. The symbolic level helps them use the Distributive Law more effectively in their computations. As we have seen earlier, what is needed is an ability to flexibly move back and forth between these levels—a binocular view.

7 • Expanding the number system

Students begin to develop the concept of number through counting, 1, 2, 3, ... As they go through school, their concept of number expands to accommodate the new kinds of numbers they encounter, first 0, and later negative numbers, fractions, and others. Each time the numbers are extended, students must figure out how the operations work for these new numbers and reconsider the generalizations they have made.

The cases in Chapter 4 of the Casebook, "Expanding the Number System," describe the issues that arise when students of different ages address the questions of how to think about zero and negative numbers as numbers. While there are persuasive reasons to include these numbers in our number system, doing so leads to complications and ultimately requires that one's understanding of *number* be reworked. Furthermore, there are generalizations we make about operations on counting numbers, some of which continue to hold for the expanded system, and some that do not.

Students in Alexandra's first-grade class, described in Case 15, are addressing the question, "Is zero really a number?" Their response to this question is somewhat guarded. "It is really a number, but it equals nothing." When Alexandra asks, "Does it [zero] matter as a number?" the class's response is, "No, not really." However, when she observes that they need to have a 0 in order to say that they have "0 days of school left," they agree: "It counts then." Zero also matters when counting birthday parties. They definitely do not want to have "0 birthday parties this year." This conversation begins to significantly challenge students' understanding of what a number is. The number 5 tells us how many animals there are in front of us. Can there be 0 animals in front of us?

Students in Cassie's class, in Case 16, "12 cats and 0 dogs," are forming number sentences from pairs of numbers that add to 12. For instance, 7 cats and 5 dogs make 12 animals. This is to be written as $7 + 5 = 12$. Then how should they deal with the combination of 12 animals that Thomas and J.T. have thought of? It has 12 cats, so how can they include the dogs? If they say that there are "0 dogs," then they will have to write 12 + 0 = 12, and that invites 0 + 12 = 12. This pushes even further against a common-sense notion of what a number is. While it is possible to accept that there are 0 cubes or animals, the process has now gone one step further. They are being asked to *add* 0 to other numbers, to combine a set that has no animals with another set that has 12 animals. Whereas Alexandra's class is using 0 as what some people would call a "placeholder," or little more than a synonym for "nothing," Cassie's class has begun to include 0 in number sentences. Writing 12 + 0 = 12 uses 0 as more than a placeholder. It is being combined with other numbers, using the operation of addition. And what does it mean to change the order of addends—to switch two sets that are combined—when one of the sets has nothing in it? The students in Cassie's class seem comfortable with this new use of 0, but as described below, historically it was a big step for our civilization to take on 0 as a number, and it represents a big step in students' understanding.

The students in Michael's fifth-grade class are beginning to encounter some of the questions implicit in the discussion in Cassie's class. He has asked them to consider the number sentence 6 × 0 = 0. This seems like a relatively innocuous request. For them, 0 has probably become accepted and established as a number that can be written down and used in relation to addition. However, multiplying 6 and 0 raises new questions. Michael's class has begun to think about multiplication in terms of an array model. But how is one to think about an array with 6 rows and 0 columns? For that matter, if they used a grouping model for multiplication, how should they make sense of "6 groups of 0 things each," or worse yet, "0 groups of 6 things each"? Even more unusual is the question of what it would mean to skip-count by 0s. Part of the problem is that as students begin to learn arithmetic of whole numbers, the underlying model is of sets of things. To add 2 and 5, we begin with sets of 2 things and 5 things. However, the notion of a set with 0 things, called the "empty set" by mathematicians, is tricky, to say the least. We are talking about a set, something *there*, which has nothing in it, so that it is *not there*. Or, is it? Again, it is one thing to accept that such a set might exist, but it is quite another thing to combine this set with other sets and base complicated ideas and processes of arithmetic on it.

The history of the use of the number 0 confirms the complexity of the issues in these cases. Many civilizations do not have a number 0 in their number systems. Some have a special symbol to indicate "nothing," but they do not combine this symbol with other numbers using the operations of arithmetic. It is possible to imagine being able to add 0 to other numbers and yet not even consider multiplying 0 by other numbers because of the new difficulties multiplication introduces. Our number system demands "full rights and responsibilities" for the number 0 because we use it in our base-10 place-value system. It is not possible to have such a system, with all its rules and algorithms for carrying out the four operations, without having a 0 that does all the things our 0 does. There was deep distrust of the idea of 0 in Europe right up through the 13th and 14th centuries. We think of our base-10 system as a great cultural achievement, but it was only accepted slowly against genuine resistance, part of which was the result of this strange notion of 0 and its central role in this number system. Certainly, we should not expect students to move quickly or easily from a wary acceptance of "0 birthdays" or "0 days of school left" to multiplying 6×0 and 0×6. Perhaps it is not so surprising that so many students say "$6 \times 0 = 6$." What may seem like a momentary lapse or a minor error may have its roots in the difficulty inherent in understanding how multiplication with 0 is even possible.

The issues in Cases 18 and 19 repeat those of Cases 15, 16, and 17 but with greater complexity. Now students are dealing with negative numbers. In Case 18, "It has basements," students in Katrina's grades 1 and 2 class are playing a game in which they draw cards indicating how many steps to move along a number line. The cards have positive and negative numbers on them, which correspond to moves along the number line. At first, the number line includes only positive numbers and 0, but it is only a matter of time before a move below the 0 occurs— to what is eventually called "zero's basement." The marker is at 2 and a student draws a $^{-}3$ card. This requires that numbers to the left of 0 must be recognized. Now, a "minus sign" is being used in two ways: one to indicate direction of motion and the other to indicate location of a new kind of number. While Katrina is pleased at how well students engage with these new ideas, she notes that younger students in her combined grades 1 and 2 class have difficulty holding onto the places on the number line that are to the left of 0. She says "I can understand why a child who needs 5 cubes to think about 5 can't think about less than 0 yet." If numbers are closely identified with sets of things, what could it possibly mean to have a negative number? A simple set-model of numbers is beginning to be challenged.

The same escalation of complexity takes place as we move to Case 19, "Does the order rule still hold?" In this case, Lucy's third-grade class is using a number line to model negative numbers. As in Katrina's class, negative numbers are being used as places on the number line and as an indication of direction of moves along the number line. In this class, a number sentence like $a + b$ is modeled by combining a move of a steps with a move of b steps, in which a and b can be positive or negative numbers, or 0. Students are discussing the question of whether order matters when addition is modeled in this way. In particular, is it true that $3 + (^{-}7) = (^{-}7) + 3$? As Elizabeth says, "You can think of it as like different distances. Like you can go 3 and then go $^{-}7$... You'll still end up there if you went $^{-}7$ and then turned around to go 3. You still end up at the same place." Then Burt supports the idea that order does not matter, by using a subtly different interpretation of $a + b$. In his interpretation, it means "Start at a and then move b steps." Burt says that "I could start at 3 or at $^{-}7$, and I would still end up at $^{-}4$ when I use the other number." Burt's assertion amounts to saying that if one person starts at 3 and moves 7 steps to the left and another person starts at $^{-}7$ and moves 3 steps to the right, then these two people end up in the same place. Note that, at this point, students' thinking is confined to testing examples.

As we saw with the number 0, the history of the use of negative numbers suggests greater complexity than one might anticipate. Negative numbers were introduced in many cultures as part of trade and to deal with debts. They were used in China in this way many thousands of years ago. One historian suggests that they were first used in Europe in the 13th and 14th centuries in order to keep track of shipments that might have shortages or excesses. If the expected number of casks of wine in a shipment was 40, then a merchant could mark down $^{-}2$ to indicate that there were only 38 and $^{+}3$ if there were 43. This would naturally lead to adding negative and positive numbers. However, it does not automatically lead to subtracting negative numbers or to multiplying them. Each of these procedures results in complications, as anyone who has tried to reason through the rules for carrying out these processes will attest to. In our modern number system, we take it for granted that we must be able to carry out all the arithmetic operations on all numbers. That is what makes our number system a system. However, negative numbers were not fully accepted as numbers until the 17th and 18th centuries. Each step in this direction has its consequences, both for the meanings of the concept of number and the meanings of the operations involved. The remarkable thing is that it all works.

The practical value of having our full set of integers, which includes 0, negative numbers, and positive numbers, is enormous. However, including these numbers in our number system is not at all a one-step process. It is important for teachers to appreciate the magnitude of the challenge to students' understanding of what numbers and operations are as they take each step toward including these numbers into the number system. By *understanding*, I mean this term in its most fundamental sense—of what these things are and how they operate together. By the word *challenge*, I mean its fullest sense of something that can be difficult but can also be thrilling, even awesome.

8 • The laws of arithmetic

While elementary and middle-school students may use models of the operations as the basis of their justifications, mathematicians start with the laws of arithmetic as the basis for a chain of deduction.

In this essay, I have referred to two different properties of the operations of arithmetic: the Distributive Law and the Commutative Law. There are other properties of operations discussed in earlier sections that we use every day, but that have no name at all. For instance, we all know that for any number A, $A \times 0 = 0$, but this property of multiplication does not have a commonly accepted name. Similarly, if we add two numbers, A and B, and obtain the number D, then we know that if we add the number A and the number $B + 1$ (which is 1 more than B), then the answer is $D + 1$, which is equal to $(A + B) + 1$. This is a formal version of one of the computational strategies discussed in Maureen's case, Case 7. While this property does not have a name, it is a logical consequence of a property that *does* have a name, the Associative Law for Addition. This law states that, for any three numbers, A, B, and C, we can add them in two different ways. One is to first add A and B, and then add the sum $(A + B)$ to C, thus forming the sum $(A + B) + C$. The second is to first add B and C, and then add the sum $(B + C)$ to A, thus forming the sum $A + (B + C)$. The Associative Law then tells us that both ways give the same answer, $(A + B) + C = A + (B + C)$.

The main reason that certain laws have names and that they are called *laws* is that they are considered by mathematicians to be the most basic concepts, in the sense that if one assumes that they are true, then one can eventually prove every other known property of the four arithmetic operations. These are the "initial links" for mathematicians in their catalog of true generalizations about the operations of arithmetic. There are nine such laws. The first five of these laws establish the validity of certain kinds of number sentences. The next two establish the existence of certain special numbers, 0 and 1. The last two establish the existence of negatives and reciprocals of given numbers. The first of these, Inverses for Addition, only holds when our number system includes the integers. The last of these, Inverses for Multiplication, only holds when our number system includes fractions:

Commutative Law of Addition
$a + b = b + a$ for any a, b

Commutative Law of Multiplication
$a \times b = b \times a$ for any a, b

Associative Law of Addition
$(a + b) + c = a + (b + c)$ for any a, b, c

Associative Law of Multiplication
$(a \times b) \times c = a \times (b \times c)$ for any a, b, c

Distributive Law
$a \times (b + c) = (a \times b) + (a \times c)$ for any a, b, c

Identity Element for Addition
$a + 0 = a$ for any a

Identity Element for Multiplication
$a \times 1 = a$ for any a

Inverses for Addition
For any number a, there is a number, called ^-a, such that $a + (^-a) = 0$.

Inverses for Multiplication
For any non-zero number a, there is a number, called $\frac{1}{a}$, such that $a \times (\frac{1}{a}) = 1$.

Among the many reasons these laws are important to mathematicians is that they represent the culmination of a process that lasted for two hundred years, one in which the concepts of number and operation, and the very foundations of mathematics, had to be articulated, clarified, and thoroughly reworked.

There is a very interesting and instructive piece of history behind this: A great deal of the power and prestige of mathematics as a discipline can be traced to the development of calculus in the 1600s, which is, in the view of many people, one of the great cultural products of Western civilization. The invention of calculus took place at the same time that many of the physical sciences were being developed, and calculus is regarded as having played an important role in the development of these disciplines. However, the success of calculus caused an enormous problem for mathematicians. While the physical sciences could justify their validity on an "empirical" basis—that they made predictions that agreed with nature—mathematicians could only hope to justify the validity of calculus, their new creation, on a strictly logical basis—that the mathematical generalizations that make the subject work can be logically deduced from a set of truths that everyone agreed on. For the first hundred years or so after calculus was invented, there were considerable disagreements among mathematicians as to what the basic concepts and logical foundations of the subject should be. By the 1800s, mathematicians realized that in order to put calculus on a sound foundation, they had to go back to their understanding of the concept of *number*. The nine laws of arithmetic were established in the mid- to late 1800s as the starting place for a solid foundation for *number*, and thereby for calculus.

There is one significant difference between the way mathematicians think about these nine laws and the way other people consider the laws. As I have emphasized, the only way for students to establish the sense and logic of the properties of the operations of arithmetic is to use the models underlying these properties. However, in their search for logically sound foundations for calculus and the rest of mathematics, mathematicians felt that even the models of our operations are too uncertain, too subjective, too informal. Thus, mathematicians *take these laws themselves as the beginning of their chain of deduction*. This works for mathematicians because of their comfort with formal and abstract statements. The truth of these laws does not rest on anything but the agreement in the community of mathematicians that they are true and will serve as the foundation. It does not mean that in mathematics, "anything goes." It only means that truth in mathematics is a logical consequence from assumptions and definitions that humans have agreed upon.

9 • Learning to make one's way around a neighborhood

A student who can only follow the procedures of arithmetic is like someone who can only make his or her way in a neighborhood by preset instructions. A student who has more extended knowledge of arithmetic not only can follow procedures but also can examine his or her actions from various points of view, consider alternative solution paths, change plans under various circumstances, and reflect on the results of past experiences.

Most mathematics educators agree that there is a crucial dimension to knowing arithmetic beyond the mastery of procedures for carrying out the four operations. The forms of this extended knowledge are difficult to specify and are given a variety of names, using such terms as *understanding* and *number sense*. In a well-known paper, in which he explores the meanings and implications of the term *number sense*, James Greeno (1991) uses a metaphor of the world of arithmetic as a neighborhood, the place where one lives, and of number sense as the quality of "knowing your way around this neighborhood." This is a way of knowing that is beyond the details of the locations of certain places or the specific routes to be taken to move among these places. It is the result of both acting in and reflecting on one's actions in a complex place.

Extending Greeno's metaphor, one might say that this way of "knowing" is about having both specific and general knowledge of places and resources, of having both a "big picture," perhaps in the form of a map in one's head, as well as a rich storehouse of personal experiences keyed to this big picture. These personal experiences are organized by this big picture, and they give it life. The big picture informs these personal experiences and is shaped by them. A student who can only follow the procedures of arithmetic is like someone who can only make his or her way around a neighborhood using preset instructions. A student who has this more extended knowledge of arithmetic cannot only follow procedures but also has a strong sense of what to expect. Such a student can examine his or her actions from various points of view, consider alternative solution paths, change plans under various circumstances, and reflect on the results of past experiences.

But how does one gain this richer, more extended knowledge of arithmetic? How does one acquire the ability to act in this world, and at the same time, learn to view one's actions from a larger perspective? To go back to the metaphor of the world of arithmetic as a neighborhood, one needs many experiences in this world, and one needs help in constructing a larger point of view from which to examine it. Neither of these is sufficient by itself. Experience alone, especially experience in which one is primarily following instructions, rarely gives the kind of larger perspective from which to view one's actions. Looking at a map of a neighborhood, even close study of the map, without direct personal experience has only limited use in learning how to make one's way around.

Within this metaphor, students who are engaged in classroom activities devoted to articulating and justifying generalizations about arithmetic are *moving around* and *looking around*, simultaneously. They are acting and observing the patterns of their actions. They are talking about the place in which they are acting, as well as their own actions in it. In their teacher, they have a guide helping them to notice significant features of the landscape.

The cases in this book illustrate students focusing on different structural features of the world of arithmetic, which help them to see and experience this world in new and more general ways. In Chapters 1 and 7, students focus on the properties of numbers—odds and evens, and factors—and how they interact with the operations of arithmetic. In Chapter 2, they focus on computational strategies and how these strategies can become portable tools that can be applied in a variety of situations. In Chapters 3, 5, and 6, students focus on the operations of arithmetic and how their properties can be described and justified. In Chapter 4, the focus is on newly defined numbers and how these new ideas can be incorporated into the number system through a series of new definitions and re-definitions.

Throughout the Casebook, we observe students as they become engaged in this world of arithmetic, taking on new challenges, puzzling through new issues. These students take on the *All* problem, learning to use representations and representative examples to justify claims about an infinite number of numbers. They learn to explicitly make generalizations that become portable tools available for application in new situations. They grapple with the difficulties around the meanings of the operations and use various models for them, discovering when to appeal to the model and when to stay at the symbolic or number level. They take on the deep question of what a number is—that it is not an isolated symbol but an element in a number *system* that combines with other numbers through the operations of arithmetic.

Virtually all of the activities described in these cases touch on computation, the traditional work of school arithmetic. Computation is one of the most important components in the world of arithmetic. In some cases, students are carrying out many computations, while in other cases, they are thinking about general principles that will give them greater facility and ease in their computations. In still other cases, they are concerned with issues that can help them make better sense of the rules and algorithms meant to make computations easier to complete. The overall goal of the activities described here is for students to learn to get around the world of arithmetic better, more flexibly, with greater assurance and carry out more fluently, with greater conviction, what they do so much of in the world of arithmetic—computation. The goals of these activities are not limited to computational fluency, however. They are also to know and understand this world of arithmetic in multiple and interconnected ways, not as a set of isolated actions to be taken but rather as an interlocking system.

Reference

Greeno, James G. (1991). Number sense as situated knowing in a conceptual domain. *Journal for Research in Mathematics Education*, 22(3), 170–218.

Related Reading

It is only in recent years that the mathematics education research community has turned attention to algebraic reasoning in the elementary grades. For this reason, there is not an established body of research to bring to the final essay of this Casebook. However, there has been a community of educators, the authors of this Casebook among them, who, in the last fifteen years, have been collaborating to study these issues. Interested readers can find some of this thinking in the following references.

- Carpenter, T.P., Franke, M.L., & Levi, L. (2003). *Thinking Mathematically: Integrating Arithmetic and Algebra in Elementary School*. Portsmouth, NH: Heinemann.

  Written for teachers' professional development, this book and accompanying video offer more examples of young students' algebraic reasoning. The authors take readers through their analysis of the cases and provide relevant mathematical exercises.

- Kaput, J., Blanton, M., & Carraher, D. (Eds.) (in press). *Employing Children's Natural Powers to Build Algebraic Reasoning in the Context of Elementary Mathematics.* Mahwah, NJ: Lawrence Erlbaum Associates.

  This forthcoming anthology will include chapters by members of the mathematics education research community who have been meeting over a number of years to study early algebraic reasoning. The authors of *Reasoning Algebraically About Operations* will have two chapters in this book.

- Rubenstein, R., & Greenes, C. (in press). *Algebra and Algebraic Thinking in School Mathematics.* Reston, VA: National Council of Teachers of Mathematics.

  The *2008 NCTM Yearbook* focuses on the teaching and learning of algebra. One chapter is written by the authors of *Reasoning Algebraically About Operations.*

- Ball, D.L., & Bass, H. (2003). Making mathematics reasonable in school. In J. Kilpatrick, W.G. Martin, & D. Schifter (Eds.), *A Research Companion to Principles and Standards for School Mathematics* (pp. 27–44). Reston, VA: National Council of Teachers of Mathematics.
- Kaput, J. (1999). Teaching and learning a new algebra. In E. Fennema & T.A. Romberg (Eds.), *Mathematics Classrooms that Promote Understanding* (pp. 133–155). Mahwah, NJ: Lawrence Erlbaum Associates.
- Schifter, D. (submitted). Representation Based Proof. In M. Blanton, D. Stylianous, & E. Knuth (Eds.), *Proof.*
- Schifter, D. (1999). Reasoning about operations: Early algebraic thinking, grades K through 6. In L. Stiff and F. Curio (Eds.), *Mathematical Reasoning, K–12: 1999 NCTM Yearbook* (pp. 62–81). Reston, VA: National Council of Teachers of Mathematics.

Recent books about policy that address elementary- and middle-school students' algebraic reasoning include:

- Conference Board of the Mathematical Sciences (2002). *The Mathematical Education of Teachers*. Providence, RI: American Mathematical Society.
- Kilpatrick, J., Swafford, J., & Findell, B. (Eds.) (2001). *Adding It Up: Helping Children Learn Mathematics.* Washington, DC: National Academy Press.
- RAND Mathematics Study Panel (2003). *Mathematical Proficiency for All Students: Toward a Strategic Research and Development Program in Mathematics Education*. Santa Monica, CA: Rand Corporation.

Other books or chapters that have influenced the authors' thinking about algebra include:

- Chazan, D. (2000). *Beyond Formulas in Mathematics and Teaching: Dynamics of the High School Algebra Classroom*. New York: Teachers College Press.
- Chazan, D., & Yerushalmy, M. (2003). On appreciating the cognitive complexity of school algebra: Research on algebra learning and directions of curricular change. In J. Kilpatrick, W.G. Martin, & D. Schifter. *A Research Companion to Principles and Standards for School Mathematics* (pp. 123–135). Reston, VA: National Council of Teachers of Mathematics.

- Coxford, A.F., & Shulte, A.P. (Eds.) (1988). *The Ideas of Algebra, K12, 1988 NCTM Yearbook* (pp. 8–19). Reston, VA: National Council of Teachers of Mathematics.
- Kieren, C. (1992). The learning and teaching of school algebra. In D. Grouws (Ed.), *Handbook of Research on Mathematics Teaching and Learning* (pp. 390–419). New York: Macmillan Publishing Company.
- Lakoff, G., & Nunez, R.E. (2000). *Where Mathematics Comes From: How the Embodied Mind Brings Mathematics Into Being*. New York: Basic Books.
- Sfard, A. (2003). Balancing the unbalanceable: The NCTM Standards in light of theories of learning mathematics. In J. Kilpatrick, W.G. Martin, & D. Schifter. *A Research Companion to Principles and Standards for School Mathematics* (pp. 353–392). Reston, VA: National Council of Teachers of Mathematics.

Made in the USA
San Bernardino, CA
24 April 2015